ALGONQUIN

ALGONQUIN

Roderick MacKay and William Reynolds

Stoddart

A BOSTON MILLS PRESS BOOK

Canadian Cataloguing in Publication Data

MacKay, Rory
  Algonquin

Includes bibliographical references.
ISBN 1-55046-088-9

1. Natural history – Ontario – Algonquin
Provincial Park – Pictorial works. I. Reynolds,
William.   II. Title.

FC3065.A4M3 1993   508.713'147   C93-093606-X
F1059.A4M3 1993

First published in 1993 by
Stoddart Publishing Co. Limited
34 Lesmill Road
Toronto, Canada
M3B 2T6
(416) 445-3333

A BOSTON MILLS PRESS BOOK
The Boston Mills Press
132 Main St.
Erin, Ontario
N0B 1T0

Winners of the
Heritage Canada
Communications Award

American Association
for State and Local History
Award Winner

Design by Gillian Stead
Typesetting by Justified Type Inc.
Printed in Singapore

The publisher gratefully acknowledges the support of the Canada Council,
Ontario Ministry of Culture and Communications, Ontario Arts Council
and Ontario Publishing Centre in the development of writing and
publishing in Canada.

Bunchberry

CONTENTS

MAP

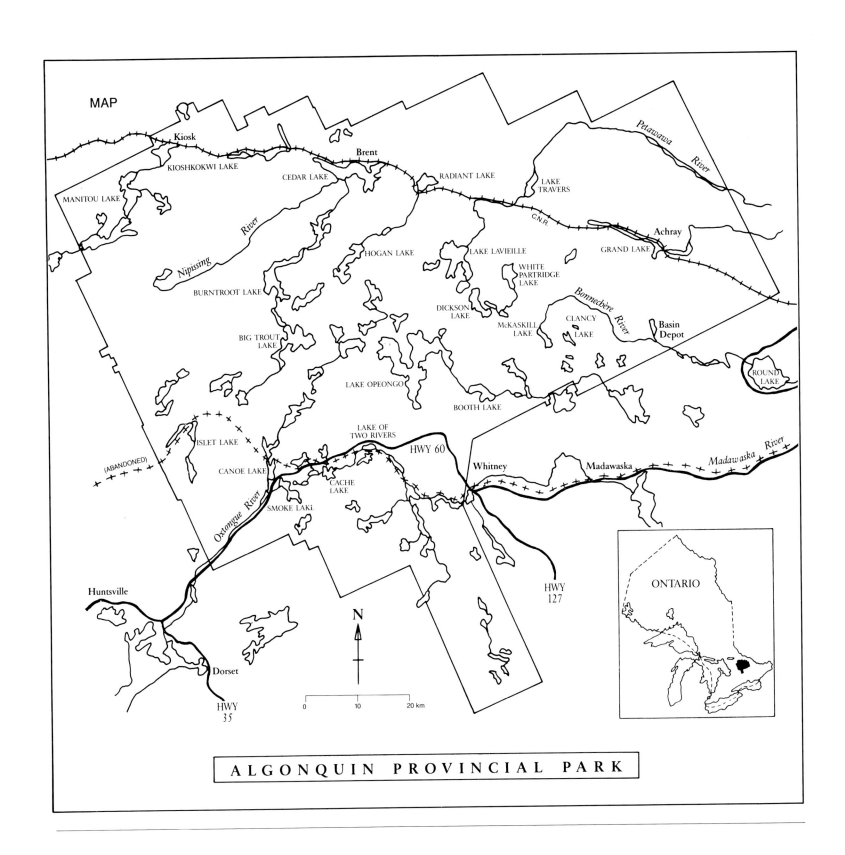

Kiosk

KIOSHKOKWI LAKE

Brent

CEDAR LAKE

RADIANT LAKE

LAKE TRAVERS

Petawawa River

MANITOU LAKE

C.N.R.

Achray

River

HOGAN LAKE

LAKE LAVIEILLE

GRAND LAKE

Nipissing

WHITE PARTRIDGE LAKE

BURNTROOT LAKE

Bonnechère River

DICKSON LAKE

CLANCY LAKE

Basin Depot

BIG TROUT LAKE

McKASKILL LAKE

ROUND LAKE

LAKE OPEONGO

BOOTH LAKE

LAKE OF TWO RIVERS

HWY 60

Madawaska River

ISLET LAKE

(ABANDONED)

CANOE LAKE

Whitney

Madawaska

CACHE LAKE

SMOKE LAKE

Oxtongue River

HWY 127

Huntsville

N

Dorset

HWY 35

0   10   20 km

ONTARIO

ALGONQUIN   PROVINCIAL   PARK

ACKNOWLEDGMENTS

I am grateful to Kate, for her patience and support. I thank my parents, Iain and Jeanne MacKay, who introduced me to Algonquin at an early age. My brother, Niall, whose advice I didn't always take but always appreciated, provided much encouragement.

I also wish to thank the following people for their contributions to the research and/or writing phases: Dan Strickland and Ron Tozer of the Algonquin Park Museum, for their support over the years and assistance checking drafts; Audrey Saunders Miller, for leading the way with *Algonquin Story*; Ottelyn Addison and Ralph Bice for their respective contributions to the historical record; The Friends of Algonquin Park, for their role in establishing an archive; Ron Pittaway and Mike Runtz, for long-lasting encouragement; John Joe Turner, for his help, friendship and belief in me; Jack Kuiak and Dan Brunton, for funding the oral history interviews of 1975 to 1977; John Denison, our publisher; Noel Hudson and Charis Wahl, my editors; Bryan and Lynn Hughes for proofreading; John and Lynne Woodman, Catherine Calvery and Bob Brooks. Many aspects of this history would still be unknown had I not had the help of Hannah Hyland, Peter McGuey, Henry McGuey, Mike Garvey, Mary Garvey, Hazel McIntyre, Emmett Chartrand, John Joe Turner and many more who told me their stories. I dedicate this book to their memory.

Special gratitude for financial support is due to The Canada Council, for two Explorations grants, and to the Royal Canadian Geographical Society, for a research grant. Thanks also to the Ontario Ministry of Natural Resources.

Finally, I thank Bill Reynolds, from whom I learned much about the value of coffee breaks, and who made a great partner.

Errors are the sole responsibility of the writer and omissions were by benevolent design only.

Roderick MacKay

I dedicate this book to Maggie, whose gentle spirit and love I have been blessed to have grace my life. Thank you to my special friends Ian Beare and Samantha Turner for their kind counsel and spiritual encouragement; to my co-author and good friend, Rory MacKay, for his steadfast enthusiasm, amiable company and patience; to Dan Strickland, Pat and Ron Tozer and all the staff of the Algonquin Provincial Park Museum for their support and happy memories; to fellow photographers Tracy Wall and Jim Waldrum, for their shared companionship; to my mother, Marion, for her understanding; to Karen Fraser and Lynn Hughes, for their infectious energy and care; to our publisher, John Denison, for patiently keeping the vision alive; to Jill Greenaway, for her care; and to Maria Valentini and Mary Mulder for their combined enthusiasm and participation.

Special acknowledgment must be given to the excellence of technical services and photographic equipment sponsorship offered to my work in North America by the staff and management of **Canon** Canada Inc.

William Reynolds

. . .what manner of place is Algonquin Park, I can only say, ''Words cannot describe it, come and see.''

INTRODUCTION

Algonquin Provincial Park sits like an island in the sea of development that is Southern Ontario. For generations people have come to Algonquin to breathe in the scent of pine woods and to play on its waters. The concept for the park originated in a report written a century ago, in 1893; since then, legislation has protected it against uses deemed inappropriate. As well, Algonquin Park owes its continued existence to the special place it occupies in the hearts of the people of Ontario — the landscape has entered the consciousness of all who have ventured there.

No one forgets that first visit to Algonquin Provincial Park. Possibly your thoughts turn to a sheltered campsite, its smooth grey rock sloping to the water's edge, hard won after a long day's paddle. Perhaps you remember the graceful white pine whispering in gentle breezes. You may recall the evening growing quieter, the water becoming still and the stars appearing through the trees at your roadside campsite. You may relive the moment when you saw your first beaver — a dark dot at the point of a silvery V in the water, which grew wider as the swimmer progressed along the shoreline. Such experiences are a part of one's own personal history of Algonquin Park.

That others enjoyed similar experiences in the near and distant past will be no surprise to you. They came by canoe up rushing rivers, by train to camps and lodges or by road to public campgrounds.

Although Algonquin is officially classified by the Ministry of Natural Resources as a Natural Environment park, the traveller in search of the sights and sounds of wild territory is seldom far from evidence of human presence on the land; indeed, human history is very much a part of the Algonquin experience. What makes Algonquin so distinctive is the blending of the natural and historic over large watersheds. Algonquin is not untracked wilderness but a place shared with past generations who have sat at the same campsites, trodden the same portages and admired the same magnificent landscapes.

The text of this book is a sampling of memories, woven into the fabric of changing times. William Reynolds has selected among the infinite images visible to the careful observer (and early riser) in this "average man's wilderness." In Algonquin these visual treasures are as likely to be right at your feet as five days' hard paddle away. Together, we — writer and photographer — celebrate the beauty and heritage of that very special place called Algonquin Park.

. . . [scenic beauty] seldom equalled in any part of our fair province.

JAMES DICKSON, 1888

1

The Algonquin Tapestry

As you drive to Algonquin Park you will find yourself moving to a higher elevation: this 7,725-square-kilometre park sits on a height of land 500 metres above sea level in the southwest and about 200 metres above sea level in the east. The edge of the Algonquin Dome, as it is called, rises gradually from the west and south; the north and east form "steps" up from the valley of the Ottawa River.

The Algonquin area has a Northern Ontario climate. The late-August heat of Toronto, Montreal and Ottawa is replaced by cool nights and misty mornings; a midwinter cool snap becomes bone-chilling cold. Here are found the shortest annual frost-free period, the lowest average daily temperature and the record low temperature for the southern part of the province. The prevailing westerly winds that sweep off Georgian Bay lose much of their moisture on the western slope of the upland area, leaving the eastern section in partial rain-shadow.

The Algonquin Dome contains the headwaters of seven major rivers: Oxtongue, South, Magnetawan, Petawawa, Amable du Fond, Bonnechere, and Madawaska. It has many small lakes, accessible only by swift-flowing streams, a significant factor in the late date of its exploration and the protection of much of it as a park, one hundred years ago.

Algonquin Park lies roughly halfway between the North Pole and the equator, in a very old section of the Earth's crust. The extensive Canadian Shield that underlies it forms part of the ancient core of the North American continent.

The Precambrian, or Canadian, Shield was formed about three and a half billion years ago. For two billion years, wind and water eroded the resistant granite. Streams and rivers carried fine mineral particles to the seas, where they settled as sandy sediments on the ocean floor. Layer upon layer, the sediments built up and turned into sandstone.

The growing continent of shield and sedimentary rock eventually collided with another land mass. The rock sediments which had been lying on the ocean floor were squeezed, pushed up and folded into a mountain range one and a half billion years ago. For millions of years, the rock sediments deep in the mountains were under extreme pressure and subjected to heat sufficient to melt them. The once-soft sedimentary rock became harder under pressure. Some rocks melted completely and recrystallized as granite; others — schist and gneiss — retained much of their fine stratification and banding. The Precambrian rocks were broadly warped upward, forming the Algonquin Arch.

Some of the rocks fractured under the pressure. Hot liquid rock flowed into the cracks, where it cooled. When the once-toffee-like rock solidified, the folds and intrusions of igneous rock were locked in place. The effect of these forces can be seen in the tortured lines of the cliffs in the Barron River Canyon or, less dramatically, in roadside rock cuts.

Gradually erosion again wore down the upland area. After as much as 20 kilometres of sediment was eroded away, the schists, granites and gneisses that were formed within the roots of the mountains were exposed — much as they are today — in the Algonquin rocks. The particles eroded from this youngest part of the shield became sediments in the seas of the Ordovician Period about 450 million years ago. The shells of sea animals added vast quantities of calcium carbonate (lime) to the ocean sediments, which built up to form the limestone deposited over the mountain roots.

Sometime in this distant past, a large meteorite crashed into the Algonquin Dome. Vaporized rock rose high in the atmosphere as the shock wave travelled outward across the bare rock. Its crater, which can be seen just north of Brent, was not recognized as such until 1951, when aerial photographs revealed its circular shape. It is thought to have been more than 850 metres deep and 4 kilometres wide, its walls as much as 100 metres higher than they are today. Shattered rock extends to a depth of 930 metres.

Seas covered the landscape. More than 200 metres of sedimentary rock — first sandstone, then limestone — was deposited in the depression of the Brent Crater. These comprise ten distinctive layers of sediment, the oldest dating back 450

Heavy masses of dark cloud are drifting athwart the heavens.
JAMES DICKSON, 1886

There is a gloomy grandeur in the natural forest. The noble pines and stately oaks bespeak the growth of centuries.
The winds sound solemnly among their branches, and the rooks caw from their hereditary nests in the tree-tops.
ALEXANDER KIRKWOOD, 1885

million years. Only the Ordovician limestone in the crater and a small section of limestone on Cedar Lake have survived subsequent erosion.

The Algonquin Dome also experienced vast sheets of glacial ice, which spread out from Canada's Arctic. The growing continental glaciers pushed southward, scraping and wearing down the sedimentry rock on the Algonquin Dome, and exposing today's resistant granitic surface.

Four times during the past million years, the glaciers advanced and retreated. Each time, a new forest grew up on the debris. At the peak of the last glacial age, ice may have been as much as 2 kilometres thick over Southern Ontario. The movement of the glacier, which retreated from this part of Ontario about twelve thousand years ago, deeply marked and scratched the hard schists and granites and dug the great depressions that formed the beds of Algonquin lakes. Valleys were filled with gravel, glacial till and debris. Vast streams flowed from the snout of the continental glacier, leaving deposits of sand, such as those we enjoy beneath the campgrounds at Lake of Two Rivers and Mew Lake.

Along the edge of the glacier, there were lakes larger than the modern Great Lakes basins. The heavy ice pushed down the surface of the Earth. As the ice melted back, the land rebounded, first in the south, and then gradually northward.

About eleven thousand years ago, the waters of glacial Lake Algonquin, to the west of the Algonquin Dome, spilled out over northern Algonquin Park, through the many-channelled Fossmill Spillway, filling these now almost empty valleys to the brim. (Thereafter the water level of Lake Algonquin dropped by about 50 metres.) The channels discharged into the glacial Champlain Sea, to the east. Such was their force that the waters, loaded with sediments, scoured the fault lines along which they flowed, exposing the great cliffs at Greenleaf Lake and in the Barron River Canyon.

The Fossmill outlet was relatively short-lived, lasting perhaps only two or three hundred years. As the ice retreated northward, the water followed the lower Ottawa outlet, leaving its legacy in the lake basins. The fish native to the Algonquin Dome, the trout, are cold-water species. Deep in the lakes along the Fossmill outlet are species of cold-water crustaceans found nowhere else nearby. Along the cliffs at Greenleaf Lake and the Barron River Canyon there are northern, western and subarctic species of ferns and flowering plants. Their ancestors were carried by the floodwaters

from hundreds of kilometres away. (The steep north-facing rock walls provide the microclimate necessary for their survival so far south.) It was on the cliffs of Greenleaf Lake that two such fern species produced a unique hybrid, discovered in the 1970s, aptly named Algonquin woodfern.

After the retreat of the ice the land was quite barren; but soon lichens, hardy herbs and shrubs, similar to those we find in bogs today, gained a foothold in sheltered locations near the leading edge of the ice sheet. It is possible to track the forest history by examining plant pollen left in the sediments of lakes. Most pollen grains are very resistant to decay. Sediments retrieved from the depths of lakes can be chemically treated to remove the less resistant material, revealing the pollen for microscopic examination. As each tree type has distinctively shaped pollen, scientists can recreate thousands of years of forest history.

Ten thousand years ago a black spruce forest dominated the cold Algonquin landscape. A slight warming period led to a forest in which red and Jack pine predominated; for three thousand years thereafter, white pine was by far the most prevalent tree. About six thousand years ago, hardwood tree species began to prevail.

For the past five thousand years, a period of slight cooling, the eastern Algonquin Dome has been an area of primarily pine growth, and the western part has been dominated by hardwoods mixed with hemlock and white pine.

Although the changes brought about by climate and other conditions are too slow to observe in one human lifespan, the forest of today is far from static. Algonquin Park lies in the transition zone between the more northerly Boreal Forest and the more southerly Great Lakes-Deciduous Forest. Microclimate conditions and soil types determine which forest has greater success on each site.

The advance and retreat of forest types may be thought of as battle manoeuvres of the conifer and broad-leaf armies. Imagine the charge of the hardwoods, their numbers and size increasing as the soil builds up and the climate warms, until they hold the upland slopes. Hemlocks hold the north slopes, and, by the lakeshore, where it is too cool for the hardwoods, the spruce and tamarack huddle, awaiting cooler times to regain their dominance.

The composition of the understory of the forest is transitional as well. Certain flowering plants are boreal; others are generally found in the deciduous forest. As the elevation increases and the average temperature drops, the climate changes significantly preclude certain flowering plants. The red trillium is abundant in the Algonquin woods in May; yet the white trillium, so common in the lands surrounding the park, is almost unknown on its upland.

Animals and birds are also influenced by vegetation types and climate. The deep snows of the area pose no difficulty for the long-legged moose, but limited the success of white-tailed deer as a native species. (Only the opening up of the forest by fire and logging, and the resultant accessible new growth, led to large deer populations in the park during the first half of this century.) Typical northern birds, such as the raven, boreal chickadee and spruce grouse mingle with species more typical of deciduous forests—the crow, the black-capped chickadee, and the ruffed grouse.

This multi-coloured tapestry of rock, water and forest has been changing slowly, season by season, for thousands of years. The arrival of a few human beings, whose ancestors may have crossed a land bridge from Siberia, made little impact on the natural order.

The woods in all their foliage have suddenly changed and assumed all the vivid tints of October, and begin to fall freely.

DAVID THOMPSON, 1837

2

THE NATIVE PEOPLES

Your canoe cuts through the mirror surface with a quiet gurgle. Mist rises softly from the water, clouding the reflection of the steep granite wall towering beside Rock Lake. Here, long ago, someone painted a crude figure on the vertical face of the rock, about head height above the water, using red ochre mixed with animal fat. No one knows for certain the age of this figure or similar markings, rare in Eastern Ontario, more common farther westward. The pictograph is a visible reminder of the first people to paddle these waters.

In the mid-1950s, C.H.D. Clarke found stone implements and a projectile point on one of the beaches at small, beach-lined Rosebary Lake, in the northwest of the park. Although the camp had been quite disturbed by later human activity, there was evidence here that red ochre pigment had been mined and ground up, perhaps for rock painting or personal adornment or to be used in burial rituals. That there was no sign of pottery at this ·site suggested the antiquity of the toolmakers and the ochre mine.

Imagine three canoes advancing down Grand Lake toward the perfect campsite, where winds disperse pesky flies, the golden beach sands are gentle underfoot and the wind through the pines lulls travellers to sleep. As the bow of the canoe touches shore, a foot descends, shifting the sand beneath it and revealing a piece of broken brown pottery. Our canoeists are not the only ones to have camped here.

Were they able to see through the ground, our modern visitors would observe more signs of human habitation. Only inorganic things remain, for weathering and acid soil have broken down all the organic material. Now, only a few stone chips, spread around all at the same level, indicate where a hunter used an antler or stone hammer to shape an arrowhead. A metre away and a few centimetres deeper lies a fish-hook, hammered from a copper nodule. Such artifacts, and the ash-coloured soil that marks a campfire, bear silent witness to the native peoples who listened to loon and wolf and watched the stars, as our modern canoeists do.

The depth at which these objects lie tells the archaeologist a history of the site. Near the surface may be a nail or rusty hinge, attesting to the presence of recent travellers. Lower down, a fragment of a clay pipe bearing a Montreal manufacturer's mark, found with stone chips and a spear point, suggests contact with traders. Below this are more stone chips and fragments of a clay pot, highly decorated, and deeper still stone tools but no pottery. Although very few if any Algonquin Park sites display all these layers of occupation, our imaginary dig, through ground and time, has turned up evidence revealing the cultures that lived in this area since the retreat of the last glacier.

The earliest known inhabitants in the park area were the Laurentian Archaic peoples. They moved east into the area as early as 5000 B.C. The Laurentian Archaic peoples used ground-slate tools and knives, but, as far as we know, no pottery. As their camps have been located along waterways and on islands, we assume that they had watercraft, probably the birchbark canoe. They hunted and fished but had no agriculture. The men secured meat, such as moose, elk, caribou, bear, beaver and fish. It is thought that the women made nets and gathered berries, nuts and other plant foods (and looked after the children).

During the Woodland Period, about 1000 B.C., pottery appeared, either because a new culture moved into the area, or because pottery-making was learned by the original inhabitants. These pottery-making people, known as the Point Peninsula culture, travelled the lakes and streams of Algonquin in small, independent family groups. The food supply available limited the population that could survive on the land. Some trade with neighbouring peoples was likely, as various pottery types have been found together. This may indicate that hunters went a considerable distance in search of wives, who brought their tribes' distinctive styles of pottery decoration to their new homes. Like earlier cultures, they traded in stone for toolmaking; chert and slate, not naturally occurring in the park area, have been found on their campsites. They may have traded with the Hurons to the west, furs and meat in exchange for corn and fishnets.

Hedgehog mushroom (dentinum repandum)

...there are great tracts of marsh and swamp,
closely grown over by stunted tamarack and
dwarf spruce, or carpeted by marsh plants...

ALEXANDER MURRAY, 1854

Burial customs of these people included the use of red ochre —
perhaps they were the ones who painted the Rock Lake pictograph.

Mike Bernard, of the Algonquins of Golden Lake, has described
the life of these pre-contact Algonquin people as following the
heartbeat of the land, the changing seasons. The people moved
into the interior each fall, leaving the lowland rivers and paddling
against the diminished autumn current of the Madawaska,
Bonnechère, Petawawa and Indian rivers toward the lakes in the
highlands. No doubt they hunted migrating waterfowl as they
travelled. It was the early autumn, too, when the lake trout
spawned on rocky beds in shallow water along the shores of lakes,
well within reach of their spears. Shortly afterward, whitefish and
speckled trout spawned, in similar locations. The fish would be
dried for the winter. Moose were hunted for their meat and hides.

Prior to freeze-up, the people would move to winter camps,
where they built wigwams of bark and skin laid over a framework
of poles. A fire in the centre of the lodge, fur robes and food
provided their only warmth during the long, dark nights of
winter. During winter little activity took place. Travel was by
toboggan and snowshoe. February and March, when the snow
was deep and the lake ice thick, was the time of famine, as stored
food was exhausted and fresh food was hard to capture.

In early spring, maple sap was collected in hollowed-out logs
or birchbark containers, then evaporated to sugar by boiling. The
sugar would be stored or traded.

Following the spring spawning of fish, winter camps in the
headwaters would be abandoned, and the people would travel

Water lily

by canoe down the cascading rivers to the lowlands along the Ottawa River, where they gathered to spend the summer.

In 1603, native people assembled on the shores of the St. Lawrence River to meet Samuel de Champlain, in whose journal we first learn of the Algonquins. (How the term "Algonquin" came to represent the peoples north and south of the Ottawa River is a matter of conjecture, for each of many groups, throughout the Ottawa Valley, had its own name. For example, the people of the Ottawa River were the Kichesippirini, those of the Madawaska River the Matouweskarini.)

During his travels up the Ottawa River in 1613 and 1615, Champlain bypassed the present park area, but referred to it as "quite a wilderness, being uninhabited except by a few Algonquin savages who dwell in the country and live by the fish they catch in the ponds and lakes with which the country is well provided."

From 1610 to 1649, the Algonquins on the Ottawa River acted as middlemen between the French and the native groups farther west, even collecting tolls for the use of their portion of the river, which was a major trade route, particularly for furs. As Iroquois lands south of Lake Ontario became depleted of furs, the Iroquois aggressively moved northward into Algonquin territory.

In 1647, the Iroquois attacked the Algonquins, Nipissings and Hurons. By 1649, few Algonquins remained. Members of the Catholic missions recorded extensive devastation of Algonquin villages along the Ottawa River when they travelled there in 1650. There is no record of the havoc wreaked on the isolated bands who had lived along the shores of the Madawaska, Bonnechère,

. . . a broad expanse of water, ruffled only with the gentle breeze that chases rippling waves along its banks, and makes panpipe music amongst its reeds and rushes.
JOSEPH ADAMS, 1912

If it can be preserved as a natural park . . . the future will prove in unmistakable terms the wisdom of guarding and improving such a reservation.

GEORGE BARTLETT, 1900

Indian, Petawawa and Amable du Fond rivers. The surviving Algonquins fled to the security of the French settlements near Quebec City and at Three Rivers. The Hurons and Nipissings fled to the west.

The Iroquois controlling Southern Ontario soon came into conflict with other tribes using the Ottawa River for commerce. Long-simmering anger at Iroquois harassment finally boiled over in the Ojibwa, including the Ottawas and Potawatamis of Lake Michigan and the Mississaugas on the north shore of Lake Huron. The Ojibwa recount that an immense force of their warriors successfully attacked the Iroquois in the 1690s, at the Saugeen River, the French River, at Lake Couchiching and in other lands they occupied. Particularly fierce fighting occurred along the Otonabee and Trent rivers, with smaller skirmishes along the Ottawa, as the Iroquois were forced to retreat from Ontario. The Ojibwa victors, later known as the Chippewa and Mississauga, occupied and settled the former lands of the Iroquois, from Georgian Bay along the shores of Lake Ontario and the Ottawa River to the Rideau and Gananoque rivers, including the area now in Algonquin Park.

Archaeological studies by William Noble in 1937 suggest that native people of relatively recent times occupied a camp-site near the Rock Lake pictograph. Nearby are rock-lined depressions that probably served as ceremonial vision pits. Here members of the community, particularly male adolescents, would pray and fast for many days, waiting for a vision, which would provide a supernatural protector. The similarity between the Rock Lake pits and rock paintings and similar features found in Ojibwa lands farther west in Ontario strongly suggest a common origin. Perhaps it was the Mississaugas who painted the Rock Lake pictograph.

Following the British defeat of the French forces in 1760, the French negotiated on behalf of their native allies. The Articles of Capitulation specifically requested that the natives "shall be maintained in the lands they inhabit; if they chuse [sic] to remain there; they shall not be molested on any pretence whatsoever. . . ."

In the Royal Proclamation of 1763, George III stated that no governor should grant surveys or sell any land beyond the boundaries of their territories "or upon any Lands whatever, which, not having been ceded to or purchased by Us as aforesaid, are reserved to the said Indians. . . ." The King suggested that all persons who had settled on these lands "forthwith remove themselves from such settlements." He further established that lands were to be purchased only by the Crown, at a public meeting or assembly of the natives.

War and the effects of European diseases had severely reduced the native population. In 1721, the few remaining Algonquins and Nipissings gathered with some Mohawks in a settlement at Lake of Two Mountains, near Oka, Quebec. From there, these few Algonquins once again seasonally travelled to the lands they had been forced to leave. In the 1820s, John McLean, a fur trader, visited natives on the Bonnechère River and described Lake Lavieille as being "in the very centre of the Algonquin hunting grounds." Only during the first half of the nineteenth century did natives move permanently up the Ottawa Valley to the lands that by then were being extensively logged, settled or unintentionally burned over.

According to Greg Sarazin of the Golden Lake Algonquins, his people willingly shared their lands with the Europeans, while maintaining their right to the land. As European settlement and exploitation transformed the valley, the Algonquins were forced from their traditional way of life. Most of the Algonquins eventually settled at Desert Lake, north of the Ottawa River; others moved to Golden Lake on the Bonnechere River. In 1854, the Desert Lake Reserve was established; Golden Lake Reserve, considerably smaller, came into being in 1864.

. . .every bend of the river unfolds some new beauty of mountain, forest or stream; while the lakes,
though not so long as those further down, are unrivalled for beauty of scenery. . .

JAMES DICKSON, 1884

3

EXPLORING THE WATERWAYS

The upland nature of the Algonquin Dome discouraged European investigations until well after the Pacific and Arctic oceans had been discovered. Throughout the fur-trade period, most Europeans had travelled up the Ottawa River, bypassing the uplands. Agricultural settlers from the south were kept away by the poor quality of the thin soil and expanses of granite. Nonetheless, travellers' narratives and diaries provide brief glimpses of particular times and places in the lands that are now the park.

The earliest known exploration reports are those of the British army engineers who ventured into this unknown land searching for a water route from the Ottawa River to Georgian Bay, over which military men and supplies could be transported. During the War of 1812, one glaring weakness in the defence of Canada had been apparent: with so much of the border with the enemy lying along the St. Lawrence River and through the Great Lakes, it was very difficult for the British to move troops and supplies without exposing them to enemy attack. One possible solution was a transportation route, ideally a canal, a considerable distance from lakes Ontario and Erie. The rivers that flowed off the Algonquin Dome in so many directions were prime candidates.

The first expedition was undertaken by Lieut. James Catty, in 1819. He travelled from Balsam Lake, on the Trent River, to the Ottawa River by way of the Madawaska River. His report, of course, does not use modern lake names, so his actual route is left somewhat to interpretation. Some have suggested a route through the current park; others support a more likely route farther south, through Grace and Farquhar lakes. We do know that Catty portaged three miles to the headwaters of the York branch of the Madawaska River, just below Bruton Township. Catty reached the Madawaska at Kaminiskeg Lake, and followed it to the Ottawa. Lieutenant Catty could not recommend the route for a canal.

When Lieut. Henry Briscoe traversed the district in 1826, he went through territory very familiar to most modern park visitors: up the Oxtongue River, through Tea Lake, Smoke Lake and, most likely, up Ragged and Big Porcupine lakes, then overland to Head Lake. From there he went down the Madawaska River, past Lake of Two Rivers and Pog Lake. He portaged to Kearney Lake and travelled through a chain of small lakes to Lake Opeongo. From there, he either went across the Bonfield-Dickson Portage to Lake Lavieille or through Proulx, Crow and Hogan lakes. He then journeyed to Lake Travers and down the Petawawa River.

When Briscoe set out in September 1826, little was known of the territory. Inquiries among natives and trappers yielded only vague information of little value. Like explorers who would follow, Briscoe had to scan the hillsides in search of carrying places, and then clear paths wide enough for the passage of his canoes and equipment.

Briscoe returned, in 1827, to retrace his former route as far as Pog Lake, and then to follow the Madawaska River to Ottawa. He agreed with Catty that the district was unsuitable for a canal route, adding: "The country through which we passed was uniformly, with a very few exceptions, of a sterile nature, the bed of the river and the banks thereof, which are generally steep, being one continued line of granite."

Not all early explorers were looking for a canal route for military purposes. Charles Shirreff (or Sherriff) of Sand Point advocated settlement of the land between the Ottawa and Georgian Bay. In 1829, his son, Alexander, twice crossed the present park district, which, Charles wrote, "forms the most important portion of Upper Canada yet to be exploited with a view to settlement."

Alexander Shirreff paddled up the Ottawa to Deux Rivières, then toward the Petawawa (then called the Nesswabic). He had been told that farther upstream was "a great extent of fertile level country" and "by following up the most westerly branch of this river, canoes could pass to the streams running in the opposite course." It took three days to reach the waters flowing into the Nesswabic, "such was the difficulty both of finding and following this almost trackless route."

After reaching Trout (now Radiant) Lake, Shirreff proceeded upstream to Cedar Lake, where he met a native and obtained a rough map of his hunting territory close to the headwaters. Continuing upstream through Catfish, Burntroot and Big Trout lakes, Shirreff traced the route to the headwaters. After he'd made one wrong turn, another native directed him to Otter (now McIntosh) Lake and provided him with a map showing the route of the Muskoka River down toward Georgian Bay.

Shirreff described the lands around this now popular and well-travelled route:

> Hardwood now appears to be the general growth wherever a view is obtained a few hundred yards inland beyond the firs and cedars, which here as in other parts of Canada, commonly skirt the waters. . . . The shores are invariably bold, though hardly ever precipitous, but rising one or two hundred feet into gentle hills, and along swelling ridges, covered with the finest hardwood, generally with a small mixture of white pine. . . . Here amidst the most enlivening scenery, there is every appearance of fertility, and both from the nature of the soil and waters, an assurance of the country being of the most healthy nature. . . . The whole of the lakes, not only here but in every part of our routes, are deep and clear. . . and they seem generally to be stocked with fish of various sorts and excellent quality.

After crossing "a miserable sinking portage," the headwaters of the Oxtongue River were reached at today's Tom Thomson Lake. He then travelled down the Oxtongue-Muskoka to Georgian Bay.

Shirreff later retraced his route to Tea Lake, then eastward by way of a chain of small lakes to the Madawaska River. The land between Tanamakoon and Lake of Two Rivers he described as "very pleasant. . .an excellent soil." He continued along the Madawaska for a short distance and then "seven or eight miles across a poor stony tract by several small lakes and rough ill-tracked portages" to Lake Opeongo. At a narrows halfway up the lake he described "a trading house belonging to the company, occupied in the hunting season," also stating that the land was "of the most fertile appearance."

Shirreff's party carried over the Bonfield-Dickson portage to Lac Clair (Dickson Lake) "a pretty piece of water, but with sterile looking shores" and on to Lake Lavieille, where he noted "some trading huts, only occupied in the winter."

The next stage of his journey took him to Lake Travers and down the Petawawa proper. He described this route as "one of the utmost difficulties for the first forty or fifty miles the river being. . .almost a constant succession of rapids. . ."

Shirreff touted the suitability of the district for agriculture:

> It is a common opinion that land without a growth of hardwood is unworthy of occupation; but this idea, though it may generally hold good farther south, should be entirely lost sight of in exploring these northern parts of Canada— the white pine frequently forms the main growth on excellent clay soils, with but a small mixture of hardwood, and sometimes none whatever. The red pine, also well known to be so abundant on the Ottawa, is by no means so infallible a sign of inferior soils as is generally asserted. . . . On the whole, everything I have seen or heard, enables me at least to state that in this, hitherto, unnoticed part of Canada, a fine habitable country will be found, to the extent of millions of acres; and I have now only to express my hope that it will, ere long, be rendered accessible to population.

Shirreff's enthusiastic summary of the agricultural potential of the area was called into question by F.H. Baddeley, who was surveying near Georgian Bay in 1835: "He has drawn too favourable an inference from level and quality of timber neglecting the more important consideration of soil which almost everywhere throughout the country appears to be excessively light and sandy and often very shallow." Despite this critique, explorations continued, with settlement in mind.

In 1837, David Thompson set out with a familiar purpose. At sixty-seven years of age, with great experience exploring western Canada, Thompson was searching for "a navigable communication between the two waters" of the Ottawa River and Lake Huron. Despite a canoe too big for the route, much rain, a mildewed tent so leaky that even his writing and drawing paper got wet, cold nights and heavy surveying equipment, he produced excellent detailed maps of his route.

Thompson travelled up the Oxtongue to Tea Lake, where his men spent two weeks building two small canoes, which would more easily pass through the narrow channels expected ahead. On September 24, Thompson noted in his journal that the temperature had dropped to freezing and ice had formed in a kettle quite distant from their fire. He reports "dense Fog to 8 a.m. then clear fine weather" and "the woods in all their foliage have suddenly changed and assumed all the vivid tints of October, and begin to fall freely. . . ." Then he added a note of melancholy. "One cannot help a sigh at such a quick change."

The party set off: two canoes carrying men and their supplies, including a large quantity of biscuits and flour, 220 pounds (100 kg) of pork, and 60 pounds (27 kg) of beef. The men in the

The heavy mists engendered by the cool night are still hanging heavily on the waters.

JAMES DICKSON, 1886

Swamp milkweed

Painted trillium

lead canoe would clear carrying places, while Thompson surveyed the lakes: Smoke, Ragged, Porcupine and Head, then down the Madawaska through Lake of Two Rivers.

Considering the time of year, one could not be surprised that Thompson found few signs of wildlife: "The whole country seems nearly destitute of living animals and birds, as well as fish. . . . In short there is a desolation or destitution of animal life in all kinds." They saw no people, except "a young indian watching for deer" at Whitefish Lake, and at Rock Lake natives in tents, perhaps on the beach campsite at the head of the lake. There they met Chaunde, an old native, from whom they obtained meat and a map of the river below, with a caution "to be careful on the rapids."

Writing later to the provincial secretary, Thompson justified his expedition with the myth of agricultural potential: "Although the examination of the Muskako [Muskoka] River for a canal was a failure; yet it brought us acquainted with a valuable tract of country for settlement. . . . Land covered with forests of a very fine growth. . . . I had an auger to bore the ground and always found among the hardwoods from 6 to 12 inches of vegetable mould beneath which is a dark yellow soil of good quality."

Setting out with David Thompson in 1837 was William Hawkins, who took a route farther north, also in search of a canal route. Hawkins travelled up the "River Magnetawang" to its source with great difficulty, owing to a canoe, which "though only drawing about 18 inches of water, had either to be towed unladen or carried probably two thirds of the last 15 miles before coming to the heighth of land. Had we passed a month earlier, the water would certainly have been much deeper." After crossing to the headwaters of the Petawawa, they found little relief, for the small stream was so overgrown that trees and branches had to be cut "before our canoe, though only four feet wide, could pass."

Eventually he reached the chain of lakes leading to Cedar Lake. At one high wall of rock along the Petawawa River, he reported paintings of "figures of various animals and other devices." The drawings of lumbering shanties at Lake Travers on his map are the earliest such record in park history.

Hawkins described the hardwoods that surrounded the lakes and the red pine that gradually became dominant as he descended the "succession of dangerous falls and rapids" that make up the lower stretch of the river toward the Ottawa. "There are four things strikingly peculiar to this section of the country; its timber is red (red pine), its soil is red (red sand and sometimes red clay) on the banks of lakes and rivers, its rock is red, and its waters are also red, deriving their colour from the soils and rocks over which they pass." Of the hardwood lands, he said, "When the portions of this province now being settled become thickly populated I have no doubt but the major part of this tract will be found fit for settlement."

During the late 1840s, a close examination of the tributaries of the Ottawa succeeded the general reconnaissance surveys. Duncan McDonell Greenfield travelled in 1847 up the Opeongo branch of the Madawaska River to Lake Opeongo, and produced a detailed map of the river-course and shoreline.

The Bonnechère River was mapped in detail by James McNaughton between 1838 and 1848. He crossed the present park boundary on August 8, 1847: "Sunday, continued on, encamped at the head of Canoe Navigation on the Bonnechere at night about 12 miles. 9th had canoe taken up to Bason, went up the river some seven or eight miles with men. . . . 11th sent men back for the luggage left by the way, employed at my field notes, rain in the morning."

During his travels he met John Egan and Alexander McDonell "on their return overland from the big opionga lake" and made note of a number of survey lines, presumably designating timber limits, which crossed his survey. He noted buildings in several places in proximity to the lumber company roads, including — on an earlier trip in 1843 — four "chantiers" belonging to Alexander McDonell, near Basin Lake. Just above Basin Lake on the Bonnechere, he noted in his fieldbook, "the farthest point at which timber was put into the Bonnechere River prior to 1848."

The Petawawa was also surveyed in 1847–48, by J.R. McDonell. A glance through McDonell's diary reveals the harsh conditions he endured while preparing this survey: in February, "chaining through water, unable to use snowshoes water over the snow"; in March, "horrible going on ice water covering snow, very cold"; in June, "Flies were almost insufferable today"; in July, "This night the fire raged through here and it was with hard work we saved our tents."

As the price of land to the south and east rose during the 1830s and 1840s, settlers turned their attention to the Ottawa-Huron tract, and the great agricultural potential claimed for it in the early surveys. The government considered the development of roads into this "back country." One of the early road surveys, made by Robert Bell, crossed in a straight line "by the magnetic compass" from the vicinity of Bytown (Ottawa) to the Muskoka River, passing through the most southerly township of Algonquin Park, Bruton.

However, Bell's Line was not chosen for construction as a Colonization Road. The route chosen — also surveyed by Bell and his assistant, Daniel Macauley, perhaps as early as 1850 — went from Farrell's Landing on the Ottawa, 220 miles (354 km),

. . . the region is one of a multiplicity of creeks and streams, forming in their progress every here and there diminutive lakes, many of them surrounded as they are by the over-arching forest, extremely beautiful.
ROYAL COMMISSION, 1893

The cool zephyrs of evening wafted from the lake invoke slumber, invite pleasant dreams and make the dawn a blessing and an inspiration.
GRAND TRUNK RAILWAY BROCHURE, 1922

to the central point of Lake Opeongo. According to A.J. Russell, the Opeongo Road "was surveyed in 1852, and in 1854 it was opened as a winter road from the settlements in the vicinity of Renfrew to its termination at Lake Opeongo — substantial bridges being built on the principal streams." However, the road was never entirely settled as intended.

The geological survey of Alexander Murray took place in 1853. With six men in three canoes, he fully explored the headwaters of the Muskoka-Oxtongue River. Like others before him, he found it necessary to build a new canoe once reaching the upper lakes, in this case Canoe Lake. From the height of land he travelled through White Trout, Longer, Burntroot and Catfish lakes to Cedar Lake.

Commenting on the potential of the land for growing crops, he noted that "the soil is everywhere exceedingly light, and although capable of growing good crops of hay and oats for a few successive seasons it would soon be exhausted. . . ."

Other surveys penetrated only a short distance into the park district. Duncan Sinclair is reported to have surveyed the Amable du Fond River to Manitou Lake in 1848. John Snow mapped the Madawaska in 1854, and Alexander Niven travelled through Bruton and Clyde townships in 1868, venturing briefly north to Pen and Galeairy lakes. But the exploration phase was complete. The many surveyors who followed mapped out timber limits and surveyed townships for settlement.

. . . the mature trees can be cut in due season to allow the next in size a chance for growth.

ALEXANDER KIRKWOOD, 1885

4

SQUARE-TIMBER AND SAWLOGS

In the 1760s, sailing vessels were the primary form of transportation. A continuous supply of wood, for construction and repair of masts and spars for merchant and military vessels, was vital to Britain's supremacy on the seas. The countries bordering the Baltic Sea provided vast quantities of pine for the British market. The thirteen American colonies were the main source of masts and spars until the American Revolution of 1776. Many United Empire Loyalists who moved north to New Brunswick and the north shore of Lake Ontario in the 1780s brought skills they had learned in the mast trade.

The wars between Britain and France that began in 1793 lasted for twenty-two years and affected the supply of European wood, increasing British dependence on New Brunswick to supply masts. Merchants reluctant to travel to British North America requested a subsidized trade. In 1795, a duty was charged on all timber entering Britain, to help pay for the war. To ensure that the cross-Atlantic source of wood was maintained, the government applied much lower duties on colonial wood than on wood from Europe. The high rate of British shipbuilding soon exhausted the supply getting through from the Baltic States, and timber shortages in Britain occurred as early as 1804.

In 1806, Napoleon set up a partial blockade of ships approaching Britain from the Baltic Sea. That year the supply of wood to Britain was lowered by one-fifth; by 1809, no supplies of timber from the Baltic could reach British ports.

Other sources of pine existed — in the Ottawa Valley and Algonquin highlands. In 1800, Philemon Wright brought a group of colonists from Massachusetts to his extensive land grant on the present site of Hull, Quebec. In 1806, Wright and his men cut a large quantity of timber, squared the logs, as was required by British buyers, and rafted them down the Ottawa and St. Lawrence rivers to the port of Quebec. There he sold his wood to the captain of a ship bound for Britain. Thousands of rafts of red and white pine would follow during the next one hundred years. Differential duties began to be reduced in 1821 and were removed by 1860, yet the colonial square-timber trade continued to grow, peaking in 1864.

The timber of the Ottawa Valley was first taken from the lands farthest downstream, closest to market. Operations gradually extended upstream into the present Algonquin Park area. In 1836, James Wadsworth was given a licence to cut pine to the source of the Bonnechère River, though whether he actually cut within the park area is uncertain. The next year, however, John Egan and Alexander McDonell were given licences to cut on the Bonnechère River, well above Round Lake. There was also timber-making at Lake Travers on the Petawawa.

By the 1840s, timber "berths" or "limits" were laid out like a patchwork quilt over the Algonquin landscape, following the rivers and stretching back 5 miles (8 km) or halfway to the next watershed, whichever was most appropriate. Berths changed hands frequently. By 1853 timber-making had reached Radiant and Cedar lakes, and beyond.

Under such pressure, the supply of large timber was decreased on the Ottawa and its tributaries. Square-timber making was very wasteful, as Samuel Strickland explained: "The square timber got out for exportation is generally in very long lengths, and as the pine tree tapers considerably, the butt end of the tree must be nearly double the diameter of the top: so that it follows as a matter of course, that to reduce the tree to the same square, the whole length of the stick nearly one fourth of the timber — and that the most valuable part — is left in the forest."

Strickland suggested making octagonal timbers, which would save more of the outer wood and enable the utilization of smaller trees. Forced by the shortage of big trees, the making of octagonal or "waney" timber began in about 1861. Square timber rafts continued to go down the Ottawa River until 1909, but the volume of wood and the number of rafts declined rapidly.

The late John Joe Turner was a direct link to those days of square-timber. He sat on his customary storytelling bench, a stone's throw from the banks of the Bonnechère River. His hands showed the wear and tear of more than seventy years of hard labour as he held the heavy broadaxe I had brought to show him. He spoke of the winter of 1912, when he worked for the Colonial

Duff Lumber Company mill at Brûlé Lake, one of a number of mills built along the railway. — ALGONQUIN PARK MUSEUM

Lumber Company in the last of the square-timber camps on the west side of Algonquin Park. The logs were hauled out by railway and the company also cut sawlogs, but John Joe was a square-timber man!

The unofficial "Boss of the Bonnechère" was the son of a timberman. John Joe respected books, but considered it important that a young historian hear about the lumber camps from someone who remembered logging before chain saws, articulated skidders, tandem log trucks and all-season gravel roads. Those men faced the massive pines with only axes and horses.

"First of all, when they'd go into the pine stands, they'd notch the tree the way they'd want it to fall. The direction of the wind was taken into consideration when deciding this. To make sure the tree wasn't damaged, you felled a lot of small trees underneath [where it would fall] to make a bed for it, because those big trees would crash down pretty hard. Well, after they'd do that they'd finish the other notch [to cut through the trunk] and down would go the tree. In the olden days you had to chop the tree down. If you sawed it down, you had to cut the end off with an axe to show if there was any rot. The saw wouldn't show it.

"The next move was to ross it, with a rossing iron. They'd pull it along like a hoe, and [the sharpened edge] would tear the bark right off. [In this way the rough bark of the tree was removed so a smooth line could be made along it.]

"Next the lineman comes along. He puts a string from one end of the log to the other and blackens the line with a combination of water and charcoal from a burnt stick. Then the lineman would get up on that log and he would walk to the centre of it. He'd reach down and pull straight up on the line, about a foot or so, and then let it go. Down comes the string on the log and makes a black line from one end to the other. He does that to both sides.

"Well, then after that they'd start to block it. They cut out channels or notches into the side of the log, right close to the depth of the line they'd made, and [using a heavy axe] they split the blocks off. That was a terrible waste of timber. A terrific waste. They'd split that off and then they'd hack it."

Score-hacking involved making shallow cuts a few inches apart so as to bring the full length of surface being cut in as far as the line. This preparatory work was done with long-handled axes from atop the log.

The side of the log was finished with a heavy broadaxe, which functioned as, and was bevelled like, a large chisel. "Now you should see these fellows with the broadaxe. They'd come up close, next to the log, and you'd see them getting down on one knee. It was quite a task to hold the axe because the handle was offset in two ways. They were real artists. The broadaxe would be really sharp; the timber side of the axe had a straight edge [the other side had all the bevel]. Now they'd go along the log and bring the axe down, smoothing off the chips all the way along. The chips would curl off, right over like that."

John Joe went on to explain how maintenance of the correct curl of the chips in front of the broadaxe ensured that the logs were properly hewed. Such work was highly skilled and usually reserved for the most experienced of the crew. Once two sides were flattened, the log was canted or rolled over and the other two sides were lined, blocked, score-hacked and hewed. Both ends were pointed slightly to facilitate movement around obstacles during the river drive, and the task was complete.

John Joe had a wealth of stories about the sawlog industry that grew up while the big pine were being cut out. Even as timber rafts continued to bypass the Chaudière Falls in Ottawa, the power of the falls was being used to drive massive circular saws and multiple "gang" saws.

The first sawmills on the Ottawa River appeared shortly after settlement began, to produce sawn wood for local markets. Gradually the Rideau and Erie canals opened access to the cities of the American seaboard, where wood was needed. The manufacture of sawn boards and thick planks provided many jobs in the mills and the woods.

By 1854, there was an influx of American money into the sawlog industry, which had been dominated by the older British-based companies. Although many of the early timber operators

Hewing with the heavy broadaxe required great skill.

— PUBLIC ARCHIVES OF CANADA 121799

The sides of the log are scored and score-hacked in preparation for the hewer. — PUBLIC ARCHIVES OF CANADA C75266

The other two sides are prepared in similar manner and hewed.

— PUBLIC ARCHIVES OF CANADA 121800

Sawlog timber was much smaller, but still required skill in getting it down.

— CHARLES MACNAMARA COLLECTION, ONTARIO ARCHIVES

The Camboose Chantier, well banked with earth to keep out winter winds. — CHARLES MACNAMARA COLLECTION, ONTARIO ARCHIVES

Inside the camboose, the scent of beans and pork mixed with the smell of wet wool and wood smoke. — PUBLIC ARCHIVES OF CANADA 25718

had managed small-scale operations, the successful sawlog companies had extensive limits. Throughout the valley, firms such as J.R. Booth, McLachlin Brothers, Gillies Brothers, Perley and Pattee, E.B. Eddy, Alex Barnet and others built mills to convert sawlogs to lumber for local use and export.

All the activity near the Ottawa sawmills had its effect on Algonquin Park. Square-timber and sawlog operators moved farther afield, reaching the headwaters of the Madawaska and Petawawa rivers in the early 1880s. Removing large trees and transporting square-timbers to Quebec or 16-foot (4.8 m) sawlogs to Ottawa required extensive co-ordination. This left a lasting imprint on the land of Algonquin: changed forests, modified and eroded streambeds, flooded shorelines and ruined buildings.

The life of the timbermen or lumbermen was hard and isolated for the better part of the year. Their upstream journey by foot, cart or canoe began about mid-October. Their first destination was the company depot, from where they and their supplies were dispersed to camps farther upstream.

A typical camp was a collection of stables, sheds and the camboose shanty, where the men slept and ate. The early shanties were crude, but provided welcome shelter from the elements. Thomas C. Keefer described a camboose shanty in 1853:

When the grove is selected, the shanty is commenced; this is built of logs, nearly square, the fire being on a raised hearth, formed of clay enclosed in a single frame of logs and placed in the middle; a longitudinal opening in the roof, over the fire, forms what serves for a chimney; a double tier of berths all round the interior gives sleeping accommodation; a wooden crane renewed when burnt through swings over the fire and suspends the family pot, tea and bake kettle. The fire, like that of a smelting furnace, is never allowed to go out, and the tea kettle sings perpetually over it.

All meals were the same for the early shantymen: split-pea gruel, salt pork and tea made from hemlock needles. Gradually black tea and other foods were added to make the menu more palatable. Henry McGuey, a former lumberman, remembered visiting a camboose shanty somewhere on the Bonnechère. "They wanted the fire to burn slowly and not make a great big blaze — just glow. They used hardwood . . . [because] the hardwood . . . would hold the fire and hold the heat. Don't forget, they used to cook in that too. They'd make home-made beans in the sand; put a big kettle right down in the hot sand and leave it there all night and you'd have lovely beans in the morning." Bread would also

The log drive was long, hard and dangerous work.
— ALGONQUIN PARK MUSEUM

Log dams, such as this one at the foot of Annie Bay, were built throughout the park. — ALGONQUIN PARK MUSEUM

be baked in iron kettles buried in the hot sand. Potatoes and turnips were welcome additions in camps close enough to be supplied by farms.

The men of the sawlog camps lived much like their predecessors in the camboose shanties. The food was more varied, as iron cook stoves replaced the open camboose fireplace about the late 1880s. The cook was very much in charge in the cookhouse, requiring silence at meals.

There were other specialized occupations in the camp. The scaler kept track of the amount of wood cut by measuring the diameter of the logs. The teamster provided the horsepower to move logs. The filer kept the men's saws sharp in the bush. The handyman worked with wood, particularly building and repairing sleighs. The blacksmith kept the metal implements in good repair, made new ones and shoed the horses. Operations in the woods were overseen throughout the winter by the clerk and foreman, under the direction of a general manager or "walking boss," responsible to the owner.

Supplies were brought in to the shanties during the "sleigh haul," over crude winter tote roads built alongside streams and rivers. Roads through marshes or wet places were built of cedar logs laid side by side in corduroy fashion. Traces of these resistant cedar roadbeds may still be seen in some parts of Algonquin Park.

Trees for sawlogs were felled by first cutting a notch with an axe and then cutting to this notch from the other side with a cross-cut saw, operated by two men. Occasionally wedges had to be placed behind the saw to keep the blade from binding. Once the tree was felled, the branches were removed by axe, and the trunk was measured and sawn off.

There was, of course, a considerable amount of waste wood, which was left on the ground. Unfortunately, as in the days of square-timber, this slash provided fuel for extensive forest fires, which destroyed both cut-over areas and prime timber lands.

Logs were skidded by horse to a landing, where they were hauled into a pile with the help of a long horse-operated chain "decking line" and pulleys. Later in the winter, the logs were loaded onto large sleighs by a crane-like "jammer," operated by the teamster and horses. The team hauled the loaded sleigh to the log dump, at the nearest body of water.

Horses couldn't haul the sleighs over all terrain: the hauling was best done downhill, working with gravity, rather than against it, wherever possible. Therefore, the hauling trails had to be carefully laid out when constructed in the autumn.

The winter snow-covered roads were packed down by large horse-drawn wooden rollers, then iced by water-tank sleighs. This work, repeated throughout the winter to maintain the surface of the road, was usually done at night, when the temperature was low. After a snowfall, the roads were cleared by horse-drawn snowploughs.

It was also important that the roads were not too steep. On a gentle downward incline the horses could keep ahead of the heavily loaded sleigh, but on a steep slope the sleigh might overrun the horses. A man was employed at each slope to maintain the hill. On a mildly steep slope, straw was strewn over the ice surface. A steeper slope called for an application of sand.

Especially steep slopes required a device called a Barrienger Brake or "crazy wheel." This series of pulleys on a sled was anchored by cable or chain to a large tree or rock. A very long cable was run through the pulleys and attached to a sleigh at the top of the slope. The action of the pulleys on the cable, controlled by two brake handles, slowed the sleigh in its descent.

Uphill grades were avoided. For the occasional short haul up an incline, the sleigh horses would be assisted by a second "fly" team hitched to the base of the sleigh tongue.

Ralph Bice of Kearney tells of a Booth operation in the 1880s near Rosebary Lake. Timbers were hauled up the Tim River and taken over the divide with a tow engine, and then dumped into the headwaters of the Magnetawan River. After a drive to Georgian Bay, the logs were shipped by boat to Montreal.

The log drive was not a haphazard event; it had to be carefully engineered and its success depended on logistics, technology and luck. Each bend in the river had to be approached perfectly or the onrushing logs would veer off through damaging rapids or into a channel, from which it would be difficult and expensive to retrieve them. The foremen who drove the rivers had to predict how the logs would move and had to construct artificial barriers or channels to control the path and flow of the logs.

There are few rivers or streams in Algonquin Park that don't show evidence of course modification. Riverbank vegetation was cut back and companies and the government spent thousands of dollars on river improvements. The concrete dams now regulating the levels of some lakes are the successors of the wooden dams that regulated the water for the log drives. River courses had to be widened and debris removed to ensure unobstructed passage. Crews of men removed rocks from the stream bed by hand, or channels were blasted with dynamite. Wooden timber or log chutes were built — often hundreds of metres long — to bypass rapids and falls or to cut off troublesome bends in the river. Chutes, glance cribs and other "improvements" were constructed in the autumn, when water levels were lowest.

At spring break-up, the water level rose behind the closed dams. When a sufficient head of water had built up, the dam gate was opened and logs that had been dumped on the ice were flushed downstream. When the water level got too low to permit a continuous flow of water and logs, the dam was closed and the

. . . forest preservation and protection is in almost every civilized country one of the most pressing and vital of economic questions.
ROYAL COMMISSION, 1893

reservoir was allowed to build up again. Dams were built on many lakes along a waterway so the logs could be moved downstream in stages. Water was occasionally diverted from one watershed to another; Jack McIntyre, a park ranger, pointed out that a dam had been built at Wabe Lake on White Partridge Creek, which diverted water through a boggy area into Redpole Lake, at the headwaters of the Bonnechère River.

Of course the rivermen accompanied the thousands of logs downstream to ensure that the logs did not jam or get stuck on the shoreline. Our images of the river drive come from folklore: rivermen in colourful woollen jackets shouting cheerfully over the roar of white water as they easily dance across churning logs. The reality was that this job required sureness of foot, bravery and tolerance of both icy water and persistent flies. When square-timber and sawlogs were being driven at the same time, the danger of a jam was increased, due to the length of the square-timbers and the number of sawlogs.

The men spent much of their time pushing and rolling stranded logs off shoreline rocks and back into the flow, using long pike poles, and thick-handled, sharp-pointed peaveys. (These sharp-pointed implements were not used on the more easily damaged square-timbers.) When a jam occurred, the rivermen risked their lives locating and quickly extricating the key log so the logs would flow again.

The equipment needed on the drive was loaded on wagons, where possible, or in "pointers," multi-purpose boats that could withstand rapids, be portaged when necessary and travel in shallow streams. (The men claimed a pointer could "float on a heavy dew.") The cook, his helpers, the pots, food and portable drive stove would travel downstream by road or river to a pre-arranged campsite close to the end of the day's drive.

Large lakes necessitated the services of a side-paddle-wheeled steam-warping tug or "alligator." The alligator could slowly tow a large boom of logs across the lake, using a cable and winch attached to a heavy anchor to pull the load along. This logging boat could be portaged over hardwood rollers, using its own winch; thus, one alligator could be used along a chain of adjacent lakes.

Square-timbers required different treatment on large rivers. Rather than being gathered in a boom, the timbers were formed into large floating cribs. A crib comprised fifteen to twenty timbers, 40 to 50 feet (12 to 15 m) long and about 25 feet (7.6 m) wide, held together with wooden pegs and traverses or crosspieces. The cribs were linked to form timber rafts, which were carried by current and sailed down the Ottawa River. At Ottawa they were again broken down into cribs to pass through the 26-foot (7.9 m) -wide slides bypassing the Chaudière Falls. Then it was on to the St. Lawrence, arriving at Quebec City in early summer.

One of the longest and most technically difficult log drives took place on the west side of Algonquin Park. It went down the Oxtongue River, which carries the waters of Smoke, Canoe and Tea lakes, to Lake of Bays and beyond. The drive was the result of the 1892 sale of pine stands near the head of Canoe Lake to the Gilmour Company of Trenton, at the mouth of the Trent River. Lake of Bays ultimately drains into Georgian Bay, but the Trent River drains into Lake Ontario. Fortunately, the two watersheds come into close proximity near Dorset, on Lake of Bays. In 1894, using a steam-operated continuous chain, logs were taken over the height of land and then dropped into a waterway dammed to flow into the lakes that form the headwaters of the Gull and Trent rivers. Log chutes were built along the rivers, and alligators pulled the logs to the continuous chain. So complex was the drive that the logs took two years to get to the mill. By that time a railway had been built through the company limits, providing a better way to transport the logs.

With the railways through Algonquin came the sawmills. One was built at Canoe Lake by the Gilmour Company by 1896. (The boilers were brought along a tote road from Dorset.) The Gilmour mill created the village of Mowat, which boasted a population of 500 in 1896. Other mills sprang up at Rain and Brûlé lakes and in the 1930s at Lake of Two Rivers (it later moved to Whitefish Lake), at Lake Travers and Kioshkokwi Lake.

The latter mill, about which grew the town of Kiosk, changed with the market for different wood. Hardwood was in great demand, particularly for plywood — it was used in the Mosquito bomber during the Second World War — and furniture. However, hardwood could not be floated down the rivers; it had to be processed in the park. Like others, the 1936 circular-saw mill at Kiosk was expanded to house a band mill; a hardwood veneer mill was added in 1949. During the 1940s, the river drives became less frequent, ending in 1959; trucks commonly hauled supplies and logs on year-round Forest Access roads. By the 1950s, chain saws were standard equipment, though not the lightweight models of today. In the 1970s, the park mills closed or were moved; the individual companies no longer cut their own wood, but were supplied by the Algonquin Forestry Authority (a Crown corporation). Logging for pine and hardwoods continues in the Algonquin forests, still a cornerstone of the regional economy.

. . . rough and rolling, traversed by frequent rocky ridges and deep glens. . .
WALTER SHANLEY, 1856

5

RAILS THROUGH THE WILDERNESS

By 1850, it was clear that a canal through the Algonquin Dome was not practicable. A railway through the rugged Ottawa-Huron Tract was inevitable.

The first railway survey of the area — across the Ottawa-Huron Tract to Georgian Bay — was organized for the government by Walter Shanley, a civil engineer, in 1856. The work was divided into two sections. A public land surveyor, B.W. Gossage, and his men were to start from Byng Inlet on Georgian Bay, travelling east. The party attached to the surveyor, Duncan Sinclair, set out from the junction of the Bonnechère and Ottawa rivers, and was to meet Gossage at the Great Opeonga Lake "in the heart of the District."

The survey was begun on October 9. Shanley reported, "It was expected on both sides, that the appointed place of rendezvous would be reached by the middle of December: and true to their calculations, on the twelfth day of that month the western party struck, just where it intended it should, the southern extremity of Opeonga Lake." The Sinclair party arrived on December 17. The men had travelled a combined total of roughly 208 miles (335 km) under harsh conditions. Shanley reported that "a line has thus been distinctly marked throughout the forest from the waters of the Ottawa to those of Lake Huron, with posts set and numbered at the end of each mile." Sinclair noted a temperature of -34°F at Lake Opeongo on December 18; at other times the thermometer froze, at temperatures below -39°F.

The report describes the topography of the land and of the forest type across the surveyed line. Sinclair, travelling up the Bonnechère River west of Round Lake, found the land "sandy, stony, and mountainous, with scarce a living tree or animal remaining from the destruction of last summer's fires." Shanley suggested that on average "this section of the Ottawa Valley . . . is not inviting for settlement." The land to the west of Lake Opeongo, the central lakes district of Algonquin, was "rough and rolling, traversed by frequent rocky ridges and deep glens, or swelling into great 'sugar loaf' hills, from whose lofty crests the vast expanse of forest can be overlooked in all directions . . . the

timber, mixed hardwood and white pine, much of the latter being of good quality." Shanley concluded that immigration to that area along a railway would "be certain to end in failure" and would place great hardships on the settlers.

In the 1870s, the government of Canada was working on a railway to join eastern provinces of the newly formed country with British Columbia, on the Pacific Coast. Rather than an easier route through American territory, which would avoid crossing 1,000 miles (1,600 km) of Canadian Shield, officials preferred to build an all-Canadian route.

The eastern terminus of the transcontinental railway would be to the southeast of Lake Nipissing, in the northwest townships of the present park — Wilkes, Biggar, Paxton and Ballantyne. (The townships were as yet unsurveyed and designated on the maps only as A, B, C and D.)

Called the Georgian Bay Branch of the Canadian Pacific Railway, the proposed route stretched from Douglas, on the Canada Central Railway, generally northwest along the valley of the Bonnechère River, then to the "Eastern Terminus of the C.P.R." at Manitou Lake, and southwest to the mouth of the French River. There, the river channel would be modified to provide harbour facilities for lake steamers.

The Canada Central Railway would connect with Ottawa & the Intercolonial Railway, which joined the Maritime provinces with Ontario and Quebec. The charter of the Canadian Pacific Railway empowered it to acquire the Canada Central Railway, thus linking the Canadian Pacific with the Maritimes.

The contract for surveying and building the Georgian Bay Branch was taken up by A.B. Foster, who was to have the line fully operational by January 1, 1880. He would find, however, that the Algonquin landscape would not yield easily.

The detailed maps and reports of the earliest surveys were likely lost in the 1916 fire at the Parliament buildings; however, a report on the initial reconnaissance was reproduced in the Renfrew *Mercury*. A letter written by Sandford Fleming to the minister of Public Works was published in 1874, as part of the newspaper's

*From what he saw he thinks there would be no
great difficulty in obtaining a fair line...*
SANDFORD FLEMING, 1874

ongoing coverage of the railway plans. Fleming reported that he had "instructed Mr. Hazelwood to walk over the country between the mouth of the French River and Pembroke" and down the Bonnechère River to Renfrew, following "as straight a course possible easterly."

His route took him along the Nipissing River, past Burntroot and Longer lakes to Lake LaMuir and Big Crow Lake. It then followed a valley through to Lake Lavieille at Dickson Lake, where a large bridge would be required. From there the line would run eastward to White Partridge Lake and down the valley of the Bonnechère to Round Lake, Golden Lake and on to Douglas.

Hazelwood reported, "The valley of the River Bonnechere from Renfrew to the Village or headwaters . . . has uniformly even surface, and there would be no difficulty in constructing a railway through it . . . . The grades and curves would be extremely easy."

The article continues:

> With regard to the country between Lake White Partridge and Pembroke, Mr. Hazelwood was prevented by the scarcity of water and the fires in the woods, in walking over the whole of this portion of the country. He however, managed to obtain a good idea of its character by canoeing along Lakes Crooked [Stratton] and Grand, as well as along the south branch of the Petawawa [Barron River] and by walking into the interior whenever the opportunity occurred . . . . From what he saw he thinks there would be no great difficulty in obtaining a fair line.

It is interesting that Hazelwood should be so positive in his report on the land between Renfrew and the Bonnechère headwaters. It was two very steep sections in the valley of the river, just downstream from the headwaters, that proved so great an obstacle that the contractor, A.B. Foster, reported that "the engineers were baffled in obtaining a fairly practicable line . . . the work on this portion of the route is so heavy as to call for some tunnelling."

The Renfrew *Mercury* reported on December 24, 1875, that "what was described as a fine level country is now discovered to comprise huge mountains of rock, immense boulders and deep ravines."

Foster requested a change to a more northerly route, perhaps because his initial bid to the government was based on 85 miles (137 km), while the surveyed route was 143 miles (230 km). In March 1876, after requests for additional funding, time extensions and significant changes to the grades and route, Foster's contract with the government was cancelled. The $41,000 spent on surveys yielded no progress on construction of the line.

The Islet Lake trestle on the Ottawa Arnprior & Parry Sound Railway in 1896. — ALGONQUIN PARK MUSEUM

The government of Canada decided instead to build the line to North Bay along the Ottawa River shore from Pembroke (north of the future park). The Canada Central had advanced to that point, bypassing the route surveyed by Foster, and reached the new terminus at Callender, on Lake Nipissing, in August 1882. Had the original route been built, the lands of the Algonquin Dome would be of considerably different character today.

The failure of the Georgian Bay Branch did not ease the pressure to open up the Ottawa-Huron Tract. The next assault came from John R. Booth, an industrialist who owned extensive timber holdings in the area, including some of the finest stands of pine. A railway would assist his access.

John R. Booth was born in Shefford County, Quebec, in 1827. After working on the Central Vermont Railway, he moved to Ottawa in 1855. Soon in logging, Booth had some of the largest timber and sawmill interests in the Empire. He financed the Canada Atlantic Railway from Alburgh Junction, Vermont, to Ottawa. The line was completed in 1882.

Ottawa provided too small a market for the railway, so in 1892 Booth began the Ottawa, Arnprior & Parry Sound line, which crossed the Ottawa-Huron Tract through Booth's timber limits.

The line followed the Bonnechère Valley to Golden Lake and crossed to the Madawaska Valley and the Division Point at the company town of Madawaska. From there the line linked locations familiar to park visitors: Rock Lake, Whitefish Lake,

The country is considerably broken by swamps and rocky ridges.
JAMES MCLEAN, 1879

Loading logs on the J.R. Booth's
Macauley Central Railway.
— PUBLIC ARCHIVES OF CANADA C26520

Lake of Two Rivers, the Madawaska valley, Cache Lake, Canoe Lake, Brûlé and Rain lakes. From there it went on to Georgian Bay at Depot Harbour, just south of Parry Sound. The total distance was 396.6 miles (634.6 km).

Despite almost insurmountable engineering difficulties, in which the hard Precambrian rock played no small part, work on the line reached the newly established Algonquin Park in 1894. It was completed in 1896, and was operational in early 1897. Soon afterward, sawmills were established adjacent to the line, at Mowat on Canoe Lake and at Whitney on Galeairy Lake.

In 1899, the Canada Atlantic Railway, owned by J.R. Booth, took over his Ottawa, Arnprior & Parry Sound Railway. Booth set up the Canada Atlantic Transit Company, using freighter steamships to deliver grain to his railhead elevators at Depot Harbour. By carrying grain along his rail line, rather than shipping through the lower Great Lakes, Booth shortened by 800 miles (1,280 km) the distance grain had to travel to get to Montreal. On the return trip, the trains transported packaged goods from New England and supplies for his camps in the park area. Where his camps were distant from the rails, he built connecting tote roads. One

such road ran from the rail line at Rain Lake all the way up to the Nipissing River.

Ernie Montgomery of Madawaska, one of the last of the Canada Atlantic engineers, explained how the trains passed each other on the single set of tracks. A strict schedule was kept, moving one train onto a siding to let an oncoming train pass. This was called a "meet," and heaven help the engineer who was off schedule. Ernie recalled a near disaster in 1917: "That was an engine that the throttle was leaking a little bit. The fireman . . . uncoupled the engine from the train and they pulled up to the water tank. The fireman . . . was taking water when the engine started to move away. . . . When he got down he found out there was nobody on the engine. The engineer was talking to someone alongside the water tank. The engine left them at McCraney. It went over the summit. It went for eight miles without anybody on it . . . down the summit and went by Brûlé Lake Station. And it stopped by a bridge there. If I'm not mistaken, they had a meet at Brûlé Lake, and the engine went by that meet. But somehow they got hold of the dispatcher at McCraney and got the other train stopped."

The Algonquin Park Station next to Highland Inn and Headquarters at Cache Lake. The platform, although overgrown, can still be seen.
— PUBLIC ARCHIVES OF CANADA C84261

By 1904, when the Canada Atlantic was taken over by the Grand Trunk Railway, six scheduled trains, including two for passengers, passed through the park each day. By 1910, as many as 120 loads of grain a day were being shipped on the railway during the summer. During the early years of the First World War, the line transported troops to eastern ports.

The Canadian National Railway took over the line in 1923. By 1933, it was decided that the extensive repairs needed on the long wooden trestle at Cache Lake would not be made. No doubt the new highway under construction through the park entered into the decision. Trains subsequently ran from Depot Harbour east to Cache Lake and from Ottawa west to Lake of Two Rivers. By 1946, the lumber mill at Lake of Two Rivers had closed, and trains came no farther west than Whitney. In 1955, the tracks from Whitney to Cache Lake were dismantled; the track from the west was abandoned and removed in 1959.

The Canada Atlantic Railway intersected with two small railways within the park. Booth's Macauley Central Railway, which ran off the main line near Madawaska 20 miles (32 km) north to Booth Lake brought logs out from the Booth limits. The Whitney &

Opeongo Railway ran about 14 miles (22.5 km) from Sproule Bay, at the south end of the St. Anthony Lumber Company's Lake Opeongo limits, to Galeairy Lake and the mill at Whitney. The current road to Opeongo Lake, and part of Highway 60, is built on the old railbed.

There were plans for other intersecting railways. The Haliburton, Whitney & Mattawa Railway was incorporated in 1899. The line was to have run from the village of Haliburton, to the Ottawa, Arnprior & Parry Sound line at Whitney and then northwest "to a point at or near the village of Mattawa, on the Ottawa River." Later plans would have placed the line a few kilometres outside the 1894 park boundary, well within the modern park. Construction was never begun.

Three additional minor railways were built in and around Algonquin Park. The first, built by the Standard Chemical Company in 1933, ran from the chemical plant at South River to a point 5 or 6 miles (8-10 km) inside the park, at the road to Winifred Lake. Hardwood logs destined for a charcoal plant and other timber for the company sawmill were hauled by horse-drawn sleigh to the railway. George Furlong, who helped build

If nothing is done for their protection or preservation, posterity will search in vain for any trace of the former haunts of the moose, caribou, red deer, beaver and other indigenous animals.

ALEXANDER KIRKWOOD, 1885

the line, said that the rails were taken up in 1938, when the railbed was converted to a truck road.

A second line was built by the Fassett Lumber Company in the 1920s, into the northwest corner of the park. A superintendent's report for Algonquin Park in 1930 mentions that "they operate a private logging railroad on which there are many heavy grades and over which as many as sixteen cars are hauled by locomotives which have seen better days." Duncan MacLulich, a biologist, said: "The sawmill company gave me a ride on their logging railway fourteen miles down to North Tea Lake. It had an articulated [Shay] engine and on some of the hills they would break the train up and take just two to four cars at a time up that part and then keep going back for the rest."

The third, and strangest in the park, was the pole railway built to haul logs south from Edgar Lake to Grand Lake. No roadbed is visible, as the railway ran on round-log rails laid directly on the ground and across frozen creeks and lakes. Jack McIntyre, former Deputy Chief Ranger at Achray, remembered seeing a garage built for the engine, which "had fallen down near the lake" and "some of the . . . old cars and the old axles down near Grand Lake. They were just rounded out so they'd run on a log." Tom Clouthier was told by fellow old-time loggers that the line had been used until the engine fell through the ice of a small lake.

During the early years of this century, attempts were made to construct the Canadian Northern Railway, a transcontinental railway rival of the Canadian Pacific. The line passes through 80 miles (130 km) of park, much of the route in territory considered impassable by earlier surveyors. It enters the park by the valley of the Indian River, follows the valley of Stratton and Grand lakes to the valley of the Petawawa River, passing Lake Travers, Radiant, Cedar and Kioshkokwi lakes before continuing northwest to North Bay.

How this route came to be chosen is a tribute to Booth's business skill. After the construction of the Canadian Pacific Railway to the West Coast, the Grand Trunk and the Canadian Northern were determined to become transcontinental, too. Needing a route from Ottawa to its proposed western road, Canadian Northern directors William MacKenzie and Donald Mann proposed to buy the Canada Atlantic Railway from J.R. Booth. Discussions were under way when the Grand Trunk announced its intentions to head for the Pacific Ocean.

Charles Melville Hays, general manager of the Grand Trunk, did not need the Canada Atlantic to complete the Grand Trunk Pacific line, but recognized its importance for competitors MacKenzie and Mann. Negotiations to buy the line from Booth began in 1902; Hays hoped the railway could be purchased for $10 million. Meanwhile, MacKenzie and Mann were having difficulty raising cash for the sale. They offered securities, but Booth demanded federal government guarantees. Prime Minister Wilfrid Laurier, who was negotiating larger-scale issues with the Grand Trunk, delayed MacKenzie and Mann, with encouragement from Booth. Hays persuaded the Grand Trunk to outbid the negotiated offer from MacKenzie and Mann, and Booth sold to the Grand Trunk for $12 to $14 million. This forced MacKenzie and Mann to find an alternative route.

Construction on the Algonquin section of their line — the Canadian Northern Ontario Railway — began in 1912 and was completed in 1915, but the company went bankrupt. The Canadian government purchased the railway in 1918, and amalgamated it with the Grand Trunk in 1923, to form the Canadian National Railway. Passenger service has been eliminated, but CN trains continue to rumble and screech through the Algonquin landscape.

All these railway lines were hard won by their financiers and by the men who blasted the rock cuts, built the trestles and scraped together the embankments. The railways built in the park opened up territory only reached previously with great difficulty. The railways both caused fires — from sparks from the wheels or the stack — and provided access for the ranger staff to put them out and patrol. The rail lines also provided access for recreational visitors, whose impact would become significant.

. . .there is every appearance of fertility, and both from the nature of the soil and waters,
an assurance of the country being of the most healthy nature. . .

ALEXANDER SHIRREFF, 1829

6

POTATOES IN THE PINES

ew park visitors associate Algonquin Park with farming, yet widely separated agricultural clearings were cut from the forest, within the present boundaries. The earliest evidence of crops dates from Hawkins's survey of 1837. On his map, downstream from the shanties at Lake Travers, Hawkins made a notation: "Potatoes planted here — stony land."

We should not be surprised that there were farms in these woods. Thomas C. Keefer, a civil engineer, reported to a parliamentary committee in 1847 that "instead of importing from the States, or teaming from great distances, this country, if cultivated should furnish the means of obtaining the timber within it."

The first farm proper, of about 15 acres (6 ha), was indicated by Greenfield on his Opeongo River survey of 1847. In his diary he wrote: "On the south side of the river is a tract of good land on which Alexander MacDougall has made a clearing for raising grain and hay for the shanties. . . ." The farm was located south of a point between MacDougall (Booth) Lake and Farm Lake.

In 1853, Alexander Murray, geologist and surveyor, reported farms associated with the lumber trade at Cedar Lake and Trout Lake. These company farms, and others scattered across the Algonquin landscape, were known as depot farms.

Farms were cleared to serve McLachlin Brothers at Big Trout Lake and Grand Lake, Phillips Lumber Company at Phillips Lake, and the Barnet Company on Burntroot Lake. Cormier's old depot was on St. Andrew's Lake. Stuart and Grier depot, near Pretty Lake, was later operated by Capt. Levi Young. The Pembroke Lumber Company had a farm on Forbes Creek. Moor's farm at Cedar Lake was later operated by Thistle and Caswell, Hawkesbury Lumber Company, and Perley and Patee, who also had farms at Galeairy Lake, White Partridge Lake and the Nipissing River. Basin Depot at Basin Lake passed through many companies, including those operated by McDonell, McLachlin, McRae and the Golden Lake Lumber Company. There were also other farms, on the Pine River and elsewhere, some of unknown ownership. At most sites there is little evidence of past occupancy.

There is little documented record of the exact nature of most of these farms, though some locations are indicated on maps. One of the earliest farms was that of the Alexander McDonell company, built at Radiant Lake in 1852, about five years after the coming of the Bonnechère Road. On the 1861 Canada Census were the farms of Andrew and Peter White, six acres under cultivation "on unsurveyed lands Petewawe"; Joshua Smith, 100 acres (40 ha) on "Petewawe Wt Partridge Creek"; William Morris, 20 acres (8 ha) on "Petewawe Big Lake"; Robert Skeid, 100 acres on "Petewawe"; Alexander McDonald, 100 acres on "Trout Lake Petewawe"; and David Moor, 80 acres (32.3 ha) on "Cedar Lake Petewawe." Township surveys record that in 1889 the farm at White Partridge Lake was about 60 acres (24.2 ha) cleared with a good occupied house, and five or six outbuildings, some holding horses and cows.

The most intriguing of the farms reported in the census was that of John Egan, recorded as 150 acres (60.7 ha) "on Little Bonecher." Most of these old farms were visible as clearings or young forest in the 1970s, but there was no clearing along the Bonnechère River of the size reported in the census.

I first learned of the farm from John Joe Turner, who had repaired dams on the river in the fall of 1910. "Being the only young lad of the bunch and raring to go hunting, they gave me a one-shot gun and a box of cartridges, and they told me to hunt partridge on this old road, that was then newly cut. I went in on the road and I came to this place where all these stones were piled around the trees, and I wondered why they should have been so. I learned later, when I got back to the camp. They had an old gentleman sit down and tell me the whole story. His grandfather had worked there many years before. With grub hoes they put in vegetables and potatoes and what have you. And naturally, it being hardwood country, they just threw grass seed and the grass seed caught very readily. . . . The barns were full of the very best hay all the time."

The census record showed that the farm had a cash value of $3,000, with 10 acres (4 ha) of oats, 6 acres (2.4 ha) of potatoes

Portrait of John Dennison, settler at Lake Opeongo, who was killed by a bear in 1881.
— ALGONQUIN PARK MUSEUM

At the narrows of Lake Opeongo lie more stone piles, built on what may have been a native campsite, and what was reported to be a trading post in 1829. Here a farm was cleared and occupied by "Captain" John Dennison in the 1870s. His was one of a handful of private clearances that looked to the lumber camps as a market.

According to Audrey Saunders, author of *Algonquin Story*, Capt. John Dennison was born in 1799 and saw military service in the Rebellion of 1837 in Lower Canada. In 1854, he settled in Bytown and later moved to Combermere, on the Madawaska River, where he kept a "stopping place" — where teamsters could obtain food and overnight accommodation for their horses and themselves — before establishing his farm at Lake Opeongo. Audrey Saunders related the testimony of Mort Finlayson, a nephew of the Captain's son John: "His two sons Harry and Jack, decided to make their clearings. Harry's was to the left of the narrows as you pass through them from the main body of the lake; Jack's to the right." Stone piles also mark the site of the latter farm, according to the late Nick Marten, on the hillside south and west of Annie Bay. [The 1881 census records John Dennison (81); younger son, Henry (37), wife, Ellen (37), children Annie (14), Henry (10), John (8), Bessy (2), Kitty (4 months); and older son John (44), his wife, Elizabeth (37), children John (16), Margaret (12), Isabella (9), Charles (7), Mary (5), Agness (3), Elizabeth (1); and two farm labourers, Robert Hudson (36) and Thomas Hudson (19).]

In 1881, it is said Captain John was killed by a black bear caught in one of his son's traps. The bear was still alive and had dragged the trap so it was difficult to see. Dennison had an axe to protect himself, but may have fallen off a log onto the bear while searching for the trap. Dennison's grandson had accompanied the old man but remained at the shore. He heard "Jackie, go home," then nothing. He hurried to the farm and returned with his father and two other men. The bear had to be killed before Dennison's body could be recovered and brought to the farm for burial near the graves of two Dennison children. Perhaps the shocking manner of the Captain's death explains why the family soon moved away.

Other early settlers were the native family Du Fond, who originally settled on Manitou Lake. When Alexander Shirreff visited Cedar Lake in 1829, he was told of the hunting territory of a native named "Map di Fong." Duncan Sinclair noted "Amable Du Font's sugar bush" on the southwest shore of Lake Kioshkokwi on his 1848 survey map of the Amable du Fond River. By the 1871 census, there was a large extended family headed by Amable Du Fond. [According to the 1871 census, Amable Du Fond (70) lived with his mother, Catherine (100), his wife,

and the rest in pasture and hay. Livestock included twelve bulls or oxen, two cows, and eight horses. The agricultural census added that 120 other horses were associated with the farm, "employed to draw timber in their respective chantiers. . . . Half again as many more horses were employed during the winter hauling supplies to the respective chantiers."

John Joe's directions to the old farm sounded simple enough: "Follow the old road up the hill from the Bonnechère River at the site of Milldam" (where a sawmill had been built in 1848). But the road was not merely overgrown, it was invisible. Many explorations later, with clues from loggers who had seen the stone piles fifteen years earlier, the Egan farm, its stone piles and second-growth trees were rediscovered near Clancy Lake in October 1979. An examination of the age of the oldest trees among the stone piles indicated that the farm had been abandoned in the late 1860s, about the time when the Egan Limits were sold.

Alexander Murray, a geologist, described a similar farm in 1853, on Kaminiskeg Lake, outside the park. "The surface on Mr. Byer's farm was at first found to be rather stoney and large boulders would occasionally interrupt the regularity of a plough furrow, but it had been considered worthy of being cleared . . . and the stones had been collected and piled in heaps on the fields, probably to be eventually used as fence walls for the protection of future crops."

It was hard work for both man and horse on depot farms such as this one at Kiosk. — ALGONQUIN PARK MUSEUM

The farm of Paddy Garvey, pioneer of the Bonnechère, as it appeared in the early 1900s. — ALGONQUIN PARK MUSEUM

Elizabeth (60), and his brother Francis (50). Children in the household were Amable (27), Basil (23), Louis (20), Alexander (18), Joseph (16), Catherine (8) and Baptiste (5). Nearby lived Ignace Du Fond (25), widow Philomine Du Fond (40), and children Elizabeth (10), Catherine (8), and Robert (5). An unnamed Du Fond infant lived with Angelic (30) and John MacDonald (30) with MacDonald children Alfred (7) and Mary Ann (3).] A surveyor in 1882 wrote: "They have an old clearing of some thirty acres on which they grow oats, beans, potatoes, turnips, and hay in abundance, all for which they get double prices from the lumber companies." By 1893, the family had a farm on Kioshkokwi and on Manitou lakes, run by Francis Du Fond, his wife, Suzanne, and his brother Ignace.

We know more about the settlers of farms along the Bonnechère Road. As early as 1847, this road ran from below Eganville, past Round Lake and the headwaters of the Bonnechère to the farms at Radiant Lake. One of the earliest to settle on the upper section of road was Patrick Garvey, an Irishman who immigrated to New York about 1852. Like many other young men of the day, Paddy headed off to the shanties of the Ottawa Valley. He soon found employment with the John Egan company on the Bonnechère. Garvey told his family that he was a hewer of pine; however, the Canada Census of 1861 lists him as a raftsman. The 1871 census describes Paddy as a "lumberer," with thirty men

living at his place, and notes that he had cut a fair amount of red and white pine on his own account.

Paddy's son Mike recalled that his father first ran a stopping place next to the rapids at the "Head of Canoe Navigation," just upstream from Couchain Lake. Paddy called it Sligo House, after his birthplace in Ireland. Meals were prepared by Mrs. MacKay, who lived in a small cookery up the road.

Sligo House eventually fell into disuse. According to Paddy's daughter Mary, by 1881 Paddy bought the Moor depot, which was being cleared down the road from Basin Depot. He is listed as "farmer" in both the 1881 and 1891 census. In a squared-timber farmhouse next to the road, Paddy and his wife raised their seven children. [The 1891 census lists Paddy (50), his wife, Augusta (24), and children James (5), Margaret (3), and Annie (1). Later children were Patrick, Martin, Mary and Michael.] Although the lumber camps provided a ready market for their vegetables, that income alone was not sufficient to raise a family. Paddy ran another stopping place, at the farm, acted as a fire ranger for the lumber companies and provided wagon transport from the camps to the nearest settlement.

The small cookery near Sligo House was eventually taken over by Ronald McDonald, a forwarder, who transported supplies into the lumber camps from the settlements down the road. By 1891, Ronald and his wife, Kate, had four children; the grave of their

The streams are of all sizes, from the tiniest to the large river capable of floating great drives of sawlogs.

T.W. GIBSON, 1896

infant son, who died in 1888, marks their small farm. [The 1891 census records Ronald MacDonald (59), his wife, Kate (30), and children John (8), Mary Agnes (5) and Annie (1). Alexander was the child who died in 1888.]

Up the road, well past the company farm at Basin Depot and the timber chutes at Robitaille Creek, High Falls and Crooked Chute, was the riverside farm and stopping place of Dennis McGuey, a tall, stout, balding man, fluent in English and French. He had cleared about 20 acres (8 ha) along the riverbank. Just upstream was a dam, which also served as a bridge across the river; it was known as Bridgedam. (Farther upstream was Milldam, where a sawmill had once stood.)

Dennis McGuey's daughter, Hannah Hyland, recalled that the Bridgedam farm, as it was known, was cleared by Hannah and James Foy and their son Frank, about 1875. When he was a young man working in the lumber camps, Dennis McGuey had taken a particular interest in James Foy's daughter Margaret and they were married in 1881. After the death of his wife, James Foy moved to Renfrew, leaving the farm to the McGueys, who were operating a stopping place there by the time of the 1881 census. There they

raised nine children. [The census for 1891 records Dennis McGuey (34), his wife, Margaret (34), and children Mary Jane (9), Frank (7), James Foy (5), Graham (3) and Hannah (1). Born later were John, Peter, Henry and Blanche. Caroline Snyder (18) was listed as "girl servant."]

Hannah explained that it was just a small shanty at first, but gradually they cleared a great deal of land and added to the original building. The stopping place had a large sleeping room for the men, a kitchen and a dining room. The McGueys' bedrooms were adjacent to the kitchen. The house was made of hewn logs, with a scoop roof like that found on camboose shanties. The inside walls were rough board; the bedrooms were wallpapered. As at other stopping places, the ceiling was whitewashed.

The sleeping room for the men was more primitive. On all the walls were bunks, piled with straw. Each man pulled one blanket over the straw and two blankets over himself. The centrally located box stove kept them warm through the long frigid nights of the Algonquin winter.

Here, as in other stopping places, the sleeping room also doubled as a bar. Liquor or "high wine" was served from a locked

cabinet in one corner. "You mixed a gallon of it with a gallon of water," said Hannah, "and by the time a man drank one or two glasses of it he was pretty high."

According to Dennis's sons, Peter and Henry, good times were had at the stopping place. "On Saturday night you'd make a party. Dad played the fiddle . . . and he had one of those roll organs . . ." "Well, my dad would serve [liquor] all the time. He didn't have to have a licence then and he used to bring a forty-five gallon drum with sixty-five over proof ninety-five. . . . He'd mix fifty-fifty, and he charged five cents a glass. He had pure high wines. . . good strong whiskey."

Sometimes things got out of hand. "My dad had lots of trouble. He had lots of fighting, yeah, he liked fighting and he got lots of it."

For men travelling on business, the twenty-five-cent meals would be charged to the company. Men not yet hired into the camps paid cash. (In those days, a man was paid about $1 for a ten-hour workday.) The fare was much the same as they got in the lumber camps, with the addition of butter, potatoes and turnips grown on the farm. At the stopping place, they ate from ceramic plates with cutlery supplied by the McGueys, rather than from the tin shanty-ware. The McGueys kept cows, horses, sheep, pigs and poultry in the outbuildings and grew wheat and hay in addition to the vegetables.

Like other settlers in the Ottawa-Huron Tract, Dennis employed himself at a diversity of occupations to ensure his family's survival. He and his sons worked for the lumber companies in the winter. They trapped bear and operated Milldam and Bridgedam for the river drive in the spring. During the summer, Dennis visited the camps to turn over the hay and other supplies in the keepovers or storage sheds. (The green hay and oats had to be turned over every two weeks or so to prevent a potentially dangerous build-up of heat.) For many years he also worked as a fire ranger. During the autumn, he harvested his crops and hunted deer. He and his brother-in-law Peter even established a small mica mine just up river, near the Milldam.

With all this activity, much of the running of the stopping place must have fallen to Mrs. McGuey, Caroline Snyder, her helper, and the children, though Dennis was the one listed in the 1881 census as the "Hotel keeper." As soon as the boys were twelve years old, they went off to work in the lumber camps. The girls had many household tasks. Hannah Hyland, Dennis's daughter, remembered knitting socks for her brothers when she was four years old. Later she assisted her mother in making tallow candles, used to supplement the coal-oil lamps. She also made soap from wood ash and animal fat, did the family laundry, baked bread, milked the cows and made butter. A major job was sweeping and

Bill McIntyre and family on their Bonnechère River farm, early 1900s.
— HAZEL MCINTYRE COLLECTION

scrubbing the dining-room and bedroom floors, which were just bare pine boards. Soap was far too precious for such use, so fine white river sand was rubbed on as an abrasive.

In about 1906, the McLachlin Company abandoned its limits on the· upper Bonnechère, taking with it the traffic for the McGueys' stopping place at Bridgedam. The family moved down to the west shore of Basin Lake, clearing a farm and building a stopping place, frame house and outbuildings. The new farm was on the road to Carcajou Creek, the route taken by men and supplies from Killaloe Station on the Grand Trunk Railway to the J.R. Booth lumber camps at Grand Lake. (Later the men building the Canadian Northern Ontario Railway along the Petawawa also used this route.)

Being close to Basin Depot meant that it was possible for the children to get some schooling for a few years, in the Basin House, home of teacher Annie Roche, daughter of Phil Roche, who ran the stopping place for McLachlin's at Basin Depot. "She wasn't a real teacher," Hannah said, "but she knew more than we did." Later, school was held in the small building that still stands to the east of Basin Creek. Peter McGuey remembered spending only a few days at school before his father insisted he be home to tend the cattle.

Relatives of the McGueys were also affected by the McLachlin pullout. William McIntyre had a farm (cleared years earlier by Jim McIntyre), 6 miles (9.6 km) upstream from the Bridgedam, next to a big marsh. Bill and his wife, Maria — a sister of Margaret McGuey — supported their family of four on the farm. [The 1891 census records William McIntyre (35), his wife, Maria (28), and children Hanna — or Annie — (7), William (4) and James (2). Jack was born later.] Bill McIntyre's youngest child, Jack, noted, "We had a few cattle and a few sheep. My father was a fire ranger. He worked at that in the summer and worked in the bush in the winter. . . . I don't know if my father sold liquor or not. . . . He may have in the early days."

In 1892, an epidemic of diphtheria raged through the surrounding camps. Hannah said, "I had a first cousin . . . six or seven years old, and he died, up at the McIntyre place. Dad used to go up in the mornings . . . and swab their throats out. All the McIntyres were all down sick in bed at the same time, and the young lad died. But mother kept sulphur on the stove all the time. Every time she gave a man a meal she boiled the dishes. Not one of us ever took it." The McIntyres moved to Round Lake about 1906, after supplies ceased to be hauled up the road.

Jack McIntyre, who later became a deputy chief ranger of Algonquin Park, knew of another family who occupied a clearing, about 15 acres (6 ha) in extent, on the west shore of Dickson Lake. "There was a set of camps down there. Some old settlers up on Big Dickson Lake — McNichol was their name. They had made a camp there and they made maple syrup there one time — I could find the old troughs they'd made for it, you know, to take the sap in . . . and they trapped."

Of the Oram family, who lived in Preston Township, less is known. Oram and his wife apparently cleared a small farm on the north shore of Oram Lake sometime before the turn of the century. [In the 1881 census, on Unorganized Territory in South Renfrew district, Madawaska East, we find record of farmer Alexander Oram (56), his wife, Matilda (34), and children Julia (15), Matilda (13) and John Henry (10). There is no exact location given.] For a while they ran a stopping place for the J.R. Booth Company; however, the land was poor for farming and the Orams soon moved to Combermere.

The settlers of the Algonquin landscape worked hard to wrestle each tiny open patch from the forest and rock. Extensive settlement, however, did not follow, and the signs of their labour are slowly fading into the underbrush.

This vast, solitary, aromatic wilderness.

T.W. GIBSON, 1896

7

DIVIDING UP THE LAND

Anyone who has walked over one of Algonquin's backpacking or self-guided trails, or who has crossed one of the park's hundreds of portages, knows that the land does not lend itself to travel in straight lines. Yet, one hundred years ago, men not only crisscrossed the park's townships in straight lines, but carefully measured as they went. A township survey was a prerequisite for opening land for settlement.

During the 1870s and '80s, there was strong pressure to open up these lands. Available arable land had been settled to the south, and immigrants were arriving each year. Efforts had been made to establish colonization roads into the Ottawa-Huron Tract. In spite of the early explorers' reports of the unsuitability of the soil for agriculture, between 1883 and 1893 surveyors were sent to divide the townships into lots of 100 acres (40 ha). These surveys provide a clear inventory of the Algonquin "wilderness" at that time.

Each survey was directed by an experienced public land surveyor, among them E. Stewart, Thomas Byrne, J.W. Fitzgerald, A. Niven, A.L. Russell, H.B. Proudfoot and Inspector of Surveys James Dickson. A typical survey party comprised the surveyor; a trained assistant; a cook, preferably a good one; and five axemen. The men would spend five or six months together on the survey; all but the surveyor were paid a daily wage.

It was expected that each man would consume 2 to 3 pounds (0.9 to 1.3 kg) of food a day. Provisions consisted largely of pork and flour for bread but also included beans, dried apples, salt, pepper, raisins, rice, currants, sugar, tea and yeast. Most of this food was packed in fifty-pound (22.6 kg) sacks.

The survey parties carried their survey instruments and far more equipment than the modern canoeist or hiker. A typical kit was described in the Ontario Land Surveyors' journal by W.R. Burke:

Five tents, all moderately small and light, made of drill, one for yourself and assistant, one for the cook and another man, one to hold four men, one for provisions etc., at camp, and another for the storage of the bulk of supplies at a point perhaps where you enter the township; eight pairs of double blankets; three or four rubber sheets are very comfortable and useful to take along; one light tarpaulin, eight leather packing straps, with headpieces to rest on head when carrying; six axes, weighing about 3 1/4 pounds each; one small axe with leather cover for head chainman; two brush hooks; one small grinding stone; some small whet stones; one ball of strong twine; ten common table knives; ten common table forks; one large carving knife; one large iron fork; one large iron spoon; ten small tin spoons; one frying pan, small size; one dozen tin plates; one iron shovel, called an Irish shovel, without handle (handle can be made at each camping place); one tin dipper; a scribe or marking iron, for marking posts with; five or six pounds of pitch for canoes; two tin pails, holding about three quarts each; two tin pans to hold bread, etc., when cut up; two wash kettles, one dozen tin tea dishes; one large tin bake dish; three bake kettles, made of heavy tin, made to fit one inside the other. If you take a reflector with you, which is a very convenient article, one or two bake kettles would do. Three oval shaped tin kettles, made to fit one inside the other, for boiling pork, making tea in, etc., etc.; towelling; some extra cotton bags; one dozen axe handles. . .

Burke advised fellow surveyors that "it is wise to take some fly oil with you in a can, and some small bottles, so as to give each man a bottle to carry with him, as the flies and mosquitoes are always troublesome in the summer." (A small fire covered with damp moss, built inside the tent, provided a smudge which encouraged insects to leave the tent.)

The crew travelled by canoe to the township to be surveyed and set up a base camp. Experienced surveyors recommended training inexperienced team members by measuring distances along an already surveyed section of the adjacent township. Then they set out to establish the boundaries of the township.

The surveyor determined the party's position with a compass, a large brass instrument complete with vertical posts along which a line could be sighted. The needle on the compass was 4 to 6 inches (10 to 15 cm) long, providing extremely accurate determination of a course. From a reference point, usually a post of a neighbouring survey, the direction of travel was resolved. The rod man would stand, with a vertical rod, along the line. The surveyor's assistant would take one end of a "chain" — individual chain links, or later a long band of steel — and head towards the rod man. The chain was 66 feet (10 m) long and divided into 100 links. Cedar marking posts were set up every 20 chains along the surveyed lines and marked for identification with the scriber. The head chainman partially cleared the line of travel as he moved through. Complete clearing was carried out by the axemen who followed.

As the surveyor advanced, he frequently took a back-sight, along the cleared line of travel: back-sighting helped to eliminate the effect of any local variation of the compass caused by ore deposits. The compasses were so sensitive that knives, axes and other metal objects had to be kept away from the compass when a sighting was being taken. Static electricity build-up on the glass of the instrument was another possible source of error. The readings had to be precise. "In reading," Burke explained, "the eye should be vertically over the end of the needle to avoid parallax and the effect of refraction of the glass. A magnifying glass may be used to aid the eye."

Of course it was also important to compensate for magnetic declination, the changing relationship between true north and magnetic north. The surveyor had to calculate declination by sighting the sun at midday or, more accurately, the North Star at night.

As the survey progressed, the camp was moved repeatedly, to be close to the line being run. Beginning in the morning, all the men carried as much as they could on their trip to the new campsite. There, the cook and an assistant set up the provisions tent and organized the kitchen area. The rest of the men set up the sleeping tents and personal gear, before continuing on the survey. One man would trek back and forth to the previous campsite to transport the rest of the provisions; this might take him several days.

The workday was long and hard. After the day's surveying was done, there were axes to be sharpened, and, for the surveyor, field notes to be written and progress indicated on the township map. According to Burke, "Order, regularity, patience and perseverance, good in all pursuits, are especially necessary for a surveyor."

Once the fieldwork was done, the team was disbanded and the surveyor returned home to write his report and draw up his final map. The reports, focusing on the characteristics of the landscape and the potential for farming, do not describe "unspoiled wilderness."

There were signs of the lumber industry everywhere. In White Township in 1887, we read of "various improvements on the river such as slides, dams, chutes, etc." In Edgar, "A wagon road leads from McKay station, on the Canadian Pacific Railway to Stuart and Grier's farm, the Petawawa being crossed on a floating bridge." In Deacon, "a fair waggon road . . . to Thistle and Caswell's farm on Cedar Lake." In Master, "The township has been lumbered over many years ago, as some of the old pine stumps are to be met with." Of Freswick, the surveyor said,

"There never was much pine in this township, but now there is scarcely any left, traces of lumbering being found in all parts of the township." In Bishop, "In this part of the township there has been a large quantity of both square timber and saw-logs taken off a number of years ago. It has been cut in a very careless and extravagant manner, the best trees only having been taken out, while there are hundreds of saw-logs and many pieces of large square timber now lying rotting at the stumps or on the skidways."

Yet many parts of the area, especially in the western sections, remained well timbered. In the township of Wilkes in 1882, the surveyor noted, "It may be worthy of remark that although the country for miles north, east, south, and, I believe, west of this township has been lumbered over for thirty years or more, not one stick has yet been cut in it for that purpose." An 1882 description of Canisbay Township at Lake of Two Rivers — now the campground and old airfield — noted that "for about three fourths of a mile north of the south branch, and extending about half a mile to the north branch, the timber is mostly red pine of a good size."

Few sections of Canada present such variety of scenery in lake, river, and woodland, as Algonquin Park.
GEORGE BARTLETT, 1900

Much of the land the surveyors crossed was burnt even to the soil. — ALGONQUIN PARK MUSEUM

Vast areas of timber had been lost to forest fires (during which even the soil burned), adversely affecting agricultural potential. An 1887 description of Anglin Township revealed, "The whole township with the exception of a few small patches has been overrun by fire at different times, destroying all the valuable timber. It is now covered with a dense growth of poplar, cherry etc." In Deacon, in 1886, "I found that about one-half of the area of the township had been overrun by a very destructive fire about eighteen or twenty years ago, destroying all the valuable timber; it is now covered in most places with a dense growth of small poplar, white birch, cherry and balsam." In Fitzgerald, 1887: "In many parts the country for miles is bare, excepting clusters of charred trees few and far between, with a crop of underbrush growing up between them." In Stratton, in the vicinity of the Petawawa River, the surveyor wrote in 1893, "Much of this part has been burnt over and denuded of its timber, so that a comparatively bald and barren landscape has taken the place of what must at one time have been beautiful natural scenery." Fully 50 percent of the surveys of townships all or partly within Algonquin Park reported that fires had burned a portion of the township. Most were in the

east of the area. Roughly 80 percent of the survey reports indicated that at least half of the land was unsuitable for growing crops.

An interesting comment occurs near the end of the report on the Township of Bishop, written in 1884 by James Dickson, the public land surveyor, "It is a matter of surprise that so few tourists and seekers after romantic scenery visit the head waters of the Muskoka-Petawawa and Madawaska Rivers. They are only a short distance from the settlement and easily accessible by canoes, and the portages on the Muskoka are of a trifling character, while every bend of the river unfolds some new beauty of mountain, forest or stream; while the lakes, though not so long as those further down, are unrivalled for beauty of scenery, and it may literally be called a sportsman's paradise. . . ."

In 1886, Dickson published *Camping in the Muskoka Region,* based on his experiences surveying the townships. The story related a fictional camping trip from Dwight, up the Oxtongue River and over the height of land; to explore the headwaters and "to attract the attention of lovers of romantic scenery to these unknown wilds." Dickson obviously knew there were better uses for the area than agriculture.

. . .deep shades are thrown across the dark water of the lake, whose proud surface mirrors to perfection
every outline of cloud or hill, tree or rock. . .
JAMES WILSON, 1893

8

THE ORIGIN OF ALGONQUIN PARK

Throughout the nineteenth century, settlement spread through the Ottawa Valley and around the Algonquin Dome. A few settlers had advanced up the rivers and crude roads. The forests were being deliberately cut and inadvertently burned. Would the watersheds soon lose their ability to regulate water flow? Would the last vestige of unsettled land be cultivated?

In 1878, Alexander Kirkwood, chief of the province's Crown Lands Department, co-authored *The Undeveloped Lands in Northern and Western Ontario* with J.J. Murphy. The intention of the book was to encourage settlement of the vast Ottawa-Huron Tract, predicting that "based on the existing ratio of population to the settled portion of Ontario, this area would represent a population of at least half a million of souls.... In this estimate only the agricultural capabilities as a means of support have been taken into consideration, but if to these were added the proceeds that would result from a full, or even partial, development . . . it would not be drawing on the imagination that this broad area . . . is capable of sustaining a million or more of people. . . ."

The book's survey reports, which truthfully portrayed the land as rocky and infertile, no doubt got Kirkwood thinking about the consequences if the land at the headwaters of the Ottawa tributaries were cleared and settled.

In 1884, Robert Phipps, the clerk of Forestry, reported on his travels across the Ottawa Valley, the major watershed of Eastern Ontario, to learn of the lumbering operations in the remote camps. He travelled part way by wagon, "equipped by filling its box with clover hay. . . . The whip is cracked, two sturdy horses are doing their best, and we are rolling, jolting and tumbling over the roughest road in the universe — up great ranges of hills, down them, over rough corduroy logways in the gullies, over rocks on the level, over great stones everywhere. The waggon rattles down a hill and rushes across a hundred boulders — you are thrown violently against your companion — you are thrown to the other side. . . . You wonder what four hours in purgatory are like — or whether the . . . stone-roller trough of torture was worse than this. . . ."

Phipps commented on the considerable amount of debris produced by road building and tree felling. "All around are spread in confusion the debris — numerous balsams cut to clear the way, piled in heaps around or scattered . . . rejected butts of logs, great tops of trees, a ready fire-road indeed should sparks in summer drought light on their inflammable surface." It seemed the general opinion that though prohibitively expensive, careful clean-up of the dead wood was possible and might diminish fires.

The clerk of Forestry examined areas already burned: "Much of this is burnt so deeply that the life-giving humus has departed; a couple of crops would probably render it barren." He suggested that if settlers were encouraged to settle on better land the destruction of valuable timber could be averted.

Phipps also stressed the importance of maintaining the forest: "There is no part of the science of forestry more beneficial than that which teaches to keep covered with forest the principal heights of land. These, especially those which are termed watersheds, when covered with extensive woods, form reservoirs which supply the sources of numerous rivers, give moisture to the numerous small lakes and watercourses which intersperse the slopes below them, and preserve throughout the whole country a fertility, invariably much impaired when the forests above are destroyed."

Concluding that a portion of the remaining forest be set aside, Phipps recommended: "There is but one territory in Ontario south of Lake Nipissing where the last scheme can be carried out, which is part of the Nipissing District, where there are between twenty and thirty townships with few or no settlers. There are also there valuable pine forests. . . . I should be glad to see this portion kept in forest, as it is one of the chief watersheds of Ontario. . . ."

In 1885, Alexander Kirkwood wrote to the Honourable Thomas Pardee, minister of Crown Lands, suggesting that the area be set apart "for the preservation and maintenance of the natural forest" as well as the preservation of "the headwaters and tributaries of the Muskoka, Petawawa, Bonnechère and

White-tailed deer

*Alexander Kirkwood, the
man with a dream.*
— ALGONQUIN PARK MUSEUM

Madawaska Rivers." Kirkwood further proposed the protection
of game from hunting and trapping: "If nothing is done for their
protection or preservation, posterity will search in vain for any
trace of the former haunts of the moose, caribou, red deer, beaver
and other indigenous animals. This forest and its foresters will
be the means of protecting them." Timber would not be cut for
private use, but a system of forestry would be put into place as
a source of revenue for the park: "The timber need not be
permitted to rot down . . . but the mature trees can be cut in
due season to allow the next in size a chance for growth."

Kirkwood stressed the importance of maintaining the headwaters of the four major rivers (Muskoka, Petawawa, Bonnechere
and Madawaska), citing the potential for downstream flooding
and the effect on climate if the lands were cleared. To this end
he proposed that the government "create the forest and define
its boundaries by statute; provide for the extinction of all existing
claims" and appoint a staff to enforce regulations.

Thomas Pardee asked Inspector of Surveys James Dickson to
travel to the area and report, particularly on the unsurveyed
townships. His report, submitted in January 1888, supported the
concept of preserving the area, both for the protection of wildlife
and to ensure a reliable water supply. He suggested that eleven
townships be included in the reservation, and that a map and
guidebook be produced to encourage appreciation of scenic
beauty "seldom equalled in any part of our fair province."

Kirkwood drafted a bill to set aside the park, in 1888. Although
still uncertain which townships would be most appropriate for

inclusion, he proposed the name "Algonkin Forest and Park."
Kirkwood also gathered what information he could regarding
other forest reserves elsewhere in the world. These papers were
eventually published in 1892.

The death of Thomas Pardee in 1889 resulted in a four-year
delay in the appointment of a committee to act on the idea of
a park. However, Kirkwood and Dickson kept up the pressure.
Dickson wrote a second report, reflecting the recommendations
of the first, to A.S. Hardy, new commissioner of Crown Lands.
Finding that there were still unsurveyed townships, Hardy sent
Dickson to gather more information on the district.

A Royal Commission, established in 1892, was charged with
making "full report respecting the fitness of certain territory in
the said Province, including the headwaters of the rivers . . . with
boundaries hereafter determined for the purpose of a Forest
Reservation and National Park; the approximate cost of establishing
and maintaining such a Park; and the ends to be attained by
creation of such a Park." Its members were Alexander Kirkwood,
senior officer of the Lands Branch; Aubrey White, assistant
commissioner of Crown Lands; James Dickson, inspector of
Surveys; Robert Phipps, clerk of Forestry; Archibald Blue, director
of Mines; and the secretary to the commission, Thomas
W. Gibson.

The commission appears to have required only two formal
meetings, on November 4, 1892, and January 3, 1893. At the latter
a report was drafted and approved. The commissioners' views
on forest importance are as valid today as then:

... forest preservation and protection is in almost every civilized country one of the most pressing and vital of economic questions. It touches the welfare of the people at many points. The experience of older countries has everywhere shown that the wholesale and indiscriminate slaughter of forests brings a host of evils in its train. Wide tracts are converted from fertile plains into arid deserts, springs and streams are dried up, and the rainfall . . . now descends the valleys in hurrying torrents, carrying all before its tempestuous flood. . . . The influence of forests upon climate is almost always beneficial, as they tend to promote its humidity and exert a tempering effect upon injurious winds; consequently the destruction of a large portion of the forest growth of a country is generally attended by a deterioration of its climate. . . . The reckless removal of the forests, such as that which has characterized the greater portion of wooded America, including our own country, may for a limited time provide such a supply in prodigal profusion, but the waste of one generation must be atoned for by the enforced economy of the next.

Evening grosbeak   *Gray jay*

Barred owl   *White-breasted nuthatch*

The report set aside eighteen townships in a roughly square block of land. The park was to be called Algonquin, after the "different tribes," including "the Nipissings, Ottawas ... Mississaugas," Algonquins and others who spoke the Algonquian language. The commissioners considered it "fitting that the name of a once great and powerful people, who ... held sway over this territory centuries ago, should bequeath their name to a part of it which is now proposed to maintain, as nearly as possible, in the condition in which it was when they fished in its waters and hunted and fought in its forests."

The commission members thought that though damaged by fire, the forests could recover with careful management. "It will be easy, as time goes on, successively to replant the portions desolated by fire or thinned by the axe, and ... to contrive that every road shall open out successive vistas of light, shade, and color, of land and water, such as no forest in North America can at present equal." Logging of pine would continue; "the rights of the holders of such licences must of course be fully respected." In fact, one licence holder — perhaps hoping for government-paid fire protection — requested that his limits be included in the forest reserve.

In summing up, the commission set out six goals: "the preservation of the streams, lakes and watercourses in the Park, and especially of the head waters of those rivers which have their sources therein"; "the maintenance of the Park in a state of nature as far as possible, having regard to existing interests; and the preservation of native forests therein and of their indigenous woods as nearly as practicable"; "to protect the fish, insectivorous and other birds, game and fur-bearing animals therein, and to encourage their growth and increase"; "to provide a field for experiments in and the practice of systematic forestry upon a limited scale"; "to serve as a sanitarium or place of health resort"; "to secure the benefits which the retention of a large block of forest would confer upon the climate and watercourses of the surrounding portions of the Province."

The Recommendations of the commission were quickly acted on. The *Algonquin Park Act* was passed by the legislature in 1893.

At various times the area of Algonquin Park was increased. Lawrence and Nightingale townships were added in 1911. The townships in the east of the modern park were added in 1914, after the government negotiated a settlement with the farmers of the Bonnechère Road: John O'Hare, Paddy Garvey, Dennis McGuey, the widowed Mrs. McDonald and their families.

Initially the government evaluated their buildings and offered compensation. Dennis McGuey carried on a considerable correspondence with the government, asking that he be permitted to stay on and continue his employment as a fire ranger or park ranger, but he and the other settlers were considered to be squatters. The research notes of Audrey Saunders show that by July 1914 the government was getting impatient. The commissioner for Crown Lands asked Superintendent Bartlett, "Could Mr. McGuey be got down to a reasonable figure for his improvements? Apparently they were valued by you or he claimed they were at $2,500. Of course, it is simply impossible to pay him such a figure as that. Do you think he could be got to take something reasonable? I think your valuation of what he has done there was $1,640." The disagreement regarding value may have arisen because Dennis had been using the Bridgedam farm as well as the Basin Lake farm, where he lived.

Eventually the report for Algonquin Park for 1914 states: "The four settlers who had squatted in the township of Guthrie have been satisfactorily settled and are leaving their places." Dennis McGuey moved to Whitney. Paddy Garvey moved to the Renfrew area, then to nearby Killaloe Station. Of the O'Hares and McDonalds, there is no record.

The remaining settlers, the Du Fonds on Manitou Lake, stayed on in the park for a short while. (Their status may have been different from that of the other squatters, as a mining patent had been issued to Ignace Du Fond in 1888.) By 1916, most of the younger Du Fonds were living in Mattawa. The government offered $1,000 in compensation and agreed to permit the Du Fonds to remain at the farm on Manitou Lake for as long as either of the elder Du Fonds survived. In 1918, Francis died, his wife moved to Mattawa and a ranger was stationed at the farm.

Algonquin Park expanded periodically, the largest recent addition being that of Clyde and Bruton townships in 1961. There have been many changes in regulation, but the intent of Alexander Kirkwood, Robert Phipps and James Dickson, to preserve the headwaters from settlement, has remained unchanged.

Near the end of the lake, in a small bay, I found another camp.

BUD CALLIGHEN, 1923

9

PATROLLING THE PARK

Once the new park was established in law, it was important that an official presence be provided in the territory. On July 21, 1893, Peter Thomson was selected to be the chief ranger, at a salary of $600 a year. He was instructed to create a headquarters in the park. Men from the vicinity — Stephen Waters of Huntsville, William Geall of Port Sydney and Tim O'Leary of Uptergrove — were hired as rangers. Also on that first trip were James Dickson (representing the commission), two carpenters, Robert Dinsmore and William Morgan, and a helper, Samuel Barr.

After travelling up the Oxtongue River, making no fewer than fifteen portages, they arrived at Canoe Lake on August 2, 1893. A particularly fine grove of balsam, spruce and pine was chosen as the site for a headquarters building. While the carpenters began construction, Thomson and Dickson set out to examine the new park and determine appropriate locations for the shelter huts from which the rangers would patrol.

Thomson described the headquarters as a "substantial, hewed log building, 21 by 28 feet, with hewed timber floor and scoop roof." There were six sleeping berths along one end of the room; a sheet-iron stove provided cooking facilities and warmth. Shortly after it was completed, when the park staff was away, the Gilmour company built a lumber camp "immediately alongside and within ten or twelve feet of ... headquarters." The company also cut down the pine in the surrounding grove, thus spoiling the aesthetic considerations for selecting that particular site.

During that first summer and fall, the rangers constructed fifteen shelter huts throughout the park, including one at Cache Lake and another at the site of Lake of Two Rivers campsite. The sites were selected so as to discourage the entry of poachers and to connect with other lakes and shelter huts. The shelter huts were 14 by 16 feet (4.2 to 4.8 m), of round logs and a handmade shingle roof. Sixteen more huts were built the following year.

A great deal of time was spent in clearing trails and waterways between the lakes in order to ease travel between shelter huts. Linen notices were nailed up around the perimeter of the park to mark the boundary.

At the request of A.S. Hardy, commissioner of Crown Lands, James Wilson, superintendent of Queen Victoria Niagara Falls Park, visited the Algonquin Park staff in late autumn. His report described access routes to the new park and some of the interior routes he followed in examining the park. He suggested that though Canoe Lake was conveniently located — connecting with waterways to the north and east, and close to the Ottawa, Arnprior & Parry Sound Railway, then under construction — a more central location would be best for the park headquarters.

Wilson commented on the beauty of the park: "On every side the forest primeval clothes the hills and mountains with verdure of varying hue down to the very shore; deep shades are thrown across the dark waters of the lake, whose placid surface mirrors to perfection every outline of cloud or hill, tree or rock; while the baby ripples from the bow of the canoe, or the congeries of air bubbles from each stroke of the paddle glisten in the sunlight like diamonds, or as the stars on a December night."

Wilson stressed the importance of the rangers. "It will be absolutely necessary for some years to come ... to [put] in a strong force of capable men as rangers or constables — men familiar with all the devious ways of trappers, who can be relied upon to faithfully carry out their instructions." In the *Algonquin Park Act*, park rangers were given the power and authority of constables. As liquor was not to be sold within the park, the rangers were also given authority under the Liquor Licence Act to seize and destroy any liquor being sold.

Wilson also suggested that the park limits be extended west to take in other townships that were little travelled.

Wilson recommended a "determined effort" to destroy wolves, and that "bears and foxes should also be destroyed without mercy." This attitude was in harmony with the original *Algonquin Park Act*, which called for a ban on hunting "except under special licence for the killing of wolves, bears, wolverines, wild cats, foxes or hawks." Rangers trapped and snared wolves in the park until the late 1950s.

One responsibility of the rangers was to keep a diary. Only a

Peter Thomson, the first superintendent of Algonquin Park. — ALGONQUIN PARK MUSEUM

Dog teams enabled rangers on this 1909 patrol to cover more territory than they could on snowshoes. — ALGONQUIN PARK MUSEUM

few have been preserved, but those of Stephen Waters and Bud Callighen reveal some sense of the life of a ranger.

During his first year as a ranger, Stephen Waters recorded trips to patrol the park, construct shelter huts and carry stoves to the shelters. He also wrote of repairing abandoned buildings of trappers and lumber companies to supplement the newly constructed shelters. The rangers also painted boats, cut miles of portages and brushed out the boundaries of the park.

Within a few years of the establishment of the park, superintendents reported an increase in the park's animal populations. Peter Thomson noted in 1894, "When I entered my duties in July 1893, scarcely a beaver sign could be seen, and it required close inspection to discover the presence of these animals. Now we are aware of at least sixty places where families of beaver have located themselves." According to John Simpson's report for 1894, "The beaver especially is multiplying in numbers. We now see many signs of them along lakes, streams and marshes where in our previous travels we could hardly perceive any, except their old works gone to wreck by reason of the beaver themselves having been killed off."

As a result of the increases, by the second decade of the park there was an attempt to make economic use of the park's animal resources. This was an aspect of changes introduced by superintendent George Bartlett, who was appointed on August 5, 1898. (Peter Thomson had died in 1894; his successor, Simpson, was replaced by Bartlett.)

During Bartlett's tenure, headquarters was moved to Cache Lake. Rangers produced maple syrup in a government-run sugar bush near Canisbay Lake. By 1909, the rangers were trapping furs for the government. In January 1911, ranger Stephen Waters wrote of setting traps in many locations, with some success: on March 17, ranger "Wattie left with 50 Beaver skins for South River to ship to Headquarters." April 15 was a notable day. He wrote: "Got a Fisher today was trying all winter to get one, quite a few of them in this section, do not seem to take bait."

Superintendent Bartlett travelled great distances by snowshoe and dog team to patrol his territory personally. Some of these trips were described in *Algonquin Story*: "It was after dark when we joined our other rangers at their shelter house. In the morning we went out with them to set traps for beaver. . . . The skins are all bailed up and taken to headquarters where they are marked Algonquin Provincial Park and stamped with the government's registered stamp — a King's Crown. . . . A great number of beaver and other furs were taken out annually representing many thousands of dollars. . . ." The government stopped using the rangers as trappers in 1920.

Bud Callighen became a ranger in 1908. Included in his papers and diaries are narrative reports of travels through the park, particularly in 1923 to 1925 when he was chief ranger under superintendents Mark Robinson and John W. Millar. During this period he and the other rangers were preoccupied with apprehending poachers, an almost impossible task, for the park was large and the staff was small. As Superintendent Mark Robinson wrote in 1923, "There are 255 miles of park border to guard with 120 miles of railroad to watch for poachers and only a staff of thirty-five, all told, to cover twenty-eight townships and nine half-townships."

Callighen wrote:

On the morning of the 13th [October 1923] portaged into Robinson Lake. Here I noticed signs of trapping and picked up three traps set for beaver. Crossing into Whiskey Jack lake found two more traps. Went into the bush travelling N.W. located a trappers camp occupied by P. Titus of Uxbridge Ont. and N. Linton of West Guilford. I placed these men under arrest. I wish here to draw the attention of the Department to the fact that these men were armed with a rifle, while I had no weapon of any kind and at the mercy of these men had they wished to use their rifle. I think the Chief Rangers should be given a good serviceable revolver or automatic, also handcuffs in addition to a good eiderdown sleeping bag for travelling as it is sometimes necessary to sleep out in the bush. These men had in their camp 16 beaver skins, 15 [Musk]rats and 1 Otter all unprime. As it was now dark we remained with the men at the camp which was merely a shelter made with poles and roofing paper. We left this camp early on the morning of the 14th Sunday and came through to Brûlé Lake. Keeping the prisoners at the Rangers' house bringing them to Headquarters by train this morning.

Most rangers had little sympathy for the poachers. As one superintendent commented, "Before the park was established, game was slaughtered in reckless fashion. . . . With the establishment of the park, poaching commenced and continues to this day. . . . In poaching, the trapper immediately starts to use all the arts of the woods and his own ingenuity to conceal his movements, the location of his traps and his work. He uses scent, works by night, comes in and out on flying trips during snowstorms, and, when cornered, does not hesitate to use firearms to threaten the ranger."

Ranger Mark Robinson, ready for winter patrol.
— ALGONQUIN PARK MUSEUM

Superintendent Bartlett, Mark Robinson, Jim Bartlett and another ranger on patrol to ensure the security of the park. — ALGONQUIN PARK MUSEUM

One of the earliest ranger cabins, in 1897. Yes, those are loon skins, apparently used for waterproof boot liners.
— ALGONQUIN PARK MUSEUM

Some years ago, a canoe was on display at the Portage Store at Canoe Lake. Painted black, it was taken from a native poacher seen in the moonlight by watchful rangers at Lake Opeongo. However, it was much harder to detect the poachers who walked to their trapping areas. These men travelled for miles along deer "runways," staying in heavily wooded areas, crossing the open burned areas or lakes only in the late evening or early morning.

Ranger Callighen followed part of a trapper trail that ran from Aylen Lake through Bonnechère Lake and on through Lake Lavieille. On Lake Clear (Dickson Lake), the trappers' sleigh trail turned north, through the woods. Callighen wrote:

From here there is a well-blazed and good trail to Hardy Bay on Lake Lavieille. . . . From Lake Lavieille I returned to the Round Island L. portage, where I met with the rest of the party. After having lunch . . . I followed the trappers

trail across Island L. to the N.W. corner picking up five mink traps set along the shore, only one mink caught. Near the end of the lake, in a small bay I found another camp. This one had been placed here since the snow and not very long ago. It was a tent only, not bush covered but evidently only temporarily vacated as there were articles of clothing left as socks, shirts, etc. also some flour, tea, tobacco, matches some traps and a 25-35 crtg. box. Some venison, also beaver, marten and mink carcasses. The tick was made of striped ticking material, similar to the one recently taken from Partridge and Vincent [trappers]. I destroyed the traps etc. carried the tent back to the other end of the lake, hiding it there. . . . From all appearances this part of the park has been a regular home for trappers for years, no ranger ever coming in there. Those rangers whose duty it is to cover that part have not done so.

There are 255 miles of park border to guard with 120 miles of railroad to watch for poachers...
MARK ROBINSON, 1923

The onset of the Great Depression led to an increase in poaching throughout the 1930s. The rangers kept up the pressure to discourage such illegal practices. However, the poachers, many of whom lived immediately around the park, continued their activities. As Emmett Chartrand put it, "You were going to sit in the house and watch your family starve, just because it was Algonquin Park?"

A trapper's life is hard at any time, but as Emmett pointed out, there were added problems when the activity was illegal. "You couldn't have a camp, you couldn't have . . . traps . . . and you were always being watched . . . sleeping on the ground, in the rain and the snow — no camp, just a tarp and a single blanket. Very little to eat. . . . You couldn't walk on a road; you never slept near a lake. . . . You learn the 'ifs and ands,' because if you don't, you don't exist. If you are in jail, who's going to keep your wife and your family?"

Joe Lavalley of Whitney recalled taking along a good axe, snowshoes, a rifle and grub, "boiled ham already cooked so you'd cut slices off it and hold it against the fire to warm it up. It would be frozen in the packsack. We never carried bread. We'd carry what we used to call a scone. . . . You'd have a slice of that and it would stay with you all day. . . . You could put four or five of them in your packsack and you were good for a whole week."

Emmett Chartrand said, "You were loaded with food going in and you were loaded with furs coming back out. So what you earned, you earned it by every drop of sweat that come off the end of your nose."

Jack Burchat, who ranged for twenty-nine years out of Basin Depot, said it was depressing to travel by snowshoe for days or weeks without seeing anyone. Even more discouraging was when you did see someone: it was always just his back as he ran away.

Bull moose

When rangers came across traps, they waited until the poacher returned. Once in late autumn, Dan Stringer and his partner waited without a fire for four days before giving up. They later learned that the poachers had already been chased out of the park by another ranger.

Max Borutski, a former ranger, recalled some poachers' tricks: "They'd tie on their snowshoes backwards and walk, trying to fool you." Once Borutski and Jack Burchat were following signs of poachers. "This was the spring of the year, the snow was all gone. . . . We got this track going up to the beaver house . . . the only place he could have been. He must have made the hole bigger and got in the beaver house and hid. I was too heavy. The darned ice wouldn't carry me, 'cause it melted all day, you see. He'd been there since twilight. . . . Burchat said 'You stay here in case he jumps out you'll catch him.' " Burchat found no sign of tracks leaving the pond; the poacher had to be in the beaver lodge. The men built a fire and stayed the night. In the morning they discovered that the ice had firmed up just enough to permit the escape of the man hiding inside.

Some poachers would sabotage the rangers' bush-line telephone system. According to Harold Hanes, a retired ranger, a poacher would cut the single wire and tie the ends tight with a piece of string. The rangers would travel along the line looking — unsuccessfully, of course — for a place where the wire was downed. It took much longer to find a concealed break than a line broken by a falling tree limb. The delay would give the poacher plenty of time to make good his escape.

Another story is told of a trapper who carved a set of wooden moose-foot stilts, on which he walked when crossing the park boundary. Poachers had to cross the boundary very stealthily after the first snowfall, as the rangers travelled the park boundary looking for snowshoe tracks — but not moose tracks. Eventually the moose-foot stilts were found, but not the trapper.

Poachers could become quite desperate when apprehended. Clarence Bouges of Dwight heard of the time "Little" Ben Sawyer of Haliburton was captured. As the rangers paddled Ben to justice, he deliberately tipped the canoe. The rangers almost drowned in the cold water and Ben's furs sank in the pack to the bottom of the lake; but without the evidence against him Ben had his freedom.

Another narrow escape was made by Norm Sawyer, also of Haliburton. One day Sawyer was on his knees skinning a beaver on a bank of the Oxtongue River. According to Clarence Bouges, the ranger Claude McFarland landed his canoe around a bend in the river and walked up behind Sawyer at the water's edge. When McFarland put his hand on the trapper's shoulder, Sawyer grabbed his arm and tossed the ranger into the river. By the time he surfaced, Sawyer and the beaver skin had disappeared into the bush.

Former park ranger Aubrey Dunne was involved in the apprehension of trappers at the Smoke Lake–Ragged Lake portage in 1936. "Fisher fur was quite valuable at that time. Maybe a nice younger fisher would be worth $125. . . . I think probably the more serious aspect of the whole thing was the Haliburton people who used to trap Algonquin Park before it was set aside as a park. Now over the years they never gave up the idea that they [had] a right in there to trap. . . . When the park was established they were told that this was a park and they were no longer permitted to trap there. They didn't take too kindly to this idea and then . . . the department deliberately had their park rangers trap for the government. Now this didn't sit too well with the Haliburton people. So, in the following years there, I would say until 1936, we used to have a lot of trouble really, in poaching with these Haliburton people. But in 1936 . . . from about the middle of October until well after Christmas, we got about eight of these Haliburton trappers, with quite large quantities of fur."

As Harold Hanes, another ranger, described it, the park rangers were tipped off that poachers would probably be using the Smoke Lake–Ragged Lake–Hollow Lake route, so eight rangers moved down to the Ragged Lake portage to wait for them. The eight poachers gathered at McIntosh Lake knew there would be rangers looking for them, but expected only a few and not a co-ordinated effort. At 2:00 a.m., when the poachers were halfway across the portage, the rangers jumped them. A scramble ensued, during which some of the poachers ran back down the trail and tried to swim for freedom across Smoke Lake.

Dan Sarazin, of the Golden Lake Algonquins, said he first trapped in the park in 1914 with his father, who had been trapping there for about fifteen years before that. Later he had his own area. When asked if the rangers ever caught him, he said: "I was in there thirty-five years, winter and summer, about six months or so. . . . Mostly all the Indians that were trappers, they had no other place to go, because that was their place to trap before they made Algonquin Park. . . . I always had the impression that [the rangers] gave us a free hand. We had no trade. We were living entirely on the fur. They knew we were there but they didn't go after us at all. . . . We had a regular snowshoe trail right up to Crow River and on the south side of Lake Lavieille."

Back when the rangers' duties included trapping, some reportedly took "one for the government and one for themself." Even after the government stopped trapping by rangers in 1920, some activity continued. In 1934, the superintendent wrote, "At various times during the Park history, rangers have gone wrong and poached fur. A ranger, if he decided to go wrong, can make a clean-up in a short time, but should be detected by his deputy. None the less, this problem in honesty has to be faced, and the only solution is to hire men who have an unblemished record for square dealing." It was suggested "that the penalties for wardens be increased to possibly five times as great as those incurred by outside poachers."

Bud Callighen wrote in his diary on January 15, 1925: "Have learned beyond doubt that the trappers who are well known to me one an ex-ranger and the other a fire ranger were assisted by ranger Grant, who kept them informed as to movements of other rangers and also took provisions in to them."

Keeping track of poachers was simplified in 1931, on the arrival of Frank A. MacDougall, Algonquin Park's first "flying superintendent." High in the sky over the park, in the Fairchild KR-34 or the De Havilland Moth, MacDougall could patrol the vast area in his care.

In his park plan of 1934, MacDougall explained that "the plane is used to look for tracks when the snow is on the ground. . . .

Red fox

Its use delimits large areas in winter by determining that there are no signs of poachers within certain sections otherwise hard to patrol, and forces the poachers to keep in the deep woods where their tracks cannot be seen, and thus makes it harder for them to travel." MacDougall also introduced dog teams because "formerly the long trips on snowshoes so tired the men that they were handicapped in dealing with poachers, who, travelling light, could make a fast run and be out before the rangers could catch up with them."

Despite all these efforts, poaching continued until 1958, when Aubrey Dunne noted, "The laying out of registered traplines and so on, pretty well . . . did away with the need or the urge to poach in the park."

Control of poaching was not the only reason to have rangers in the park. Alvin Dunne, Aubrey's brother, was a fire ranger, employed by the Ontario Forestry Board. (Fire and park rangers came under common supervision in 1930.) "We were given a canoe, a packsack, blankets and some things for ordinary living in the woods. We were assigned to a certain beat. . . . Our duty was to go over the portages and trails, and as the summer growth advanced we were expected to mow out certain areas. Old roads were kept open . . . for lines of transportation, maybe with horse and wagon or men carrying fire-fighting equipment and food. It was very primitive. . . . About all you could carry was an axe, a grub hoe and a shovel. A grub hoe was a tool for scraping away the duff down to mineral soil and making a path. . . . The first pumps we had were fairly heavy. They used two poles on each side with a man in front and a man behind. Then men would carry five lengths of hose on their backs. They'd have 500 feet [152.4 m] of linen hose. The couplings were brass and were packed in. . . . Everything was carried."

Dr. W.C. Leggett used the same primitive equipment when he was a fire ranger. "It was really wonderful what you could do with that. Especially early in the morning or late at night after the winds had gone down. There usually was a prevailing wind . . . all the day, and during that time it was pretty rough work. . . . May was the worst time for fires." Aubrey Dunne recalled, "In the summertime our main preoccupation was of course forest protection, suppression of forest fires. . . . We used to have a lot of them at times too. During those Depression years . . . we had a lot of fires deliberately set, you know, to create employment."

Aubrey Dunne first worked in the park during the summer of 1922, as a fire ranger at Big Trout Lake. There was a steel fire tower there from which fires could be spotted, particularly during dry spells and after lightning storms. Later, at Smoke Lake, where there was no steel tower, he and a partner built a wooden framework on top of a large pine tree near the shore, which served for many years as a fire tower. Wooden and, later, steel towers were built throughout Ontario on high points of land. In the park, there was one for every few townships. The towerman lived in a ranger cabin near the base during the spring and summer. Up in the small cupola, 100 feet (30 m) above the ground, was a round table on which there was a map and a large device by which a compass bearing could be determined. All the walls contained large windows, through which "a smoke" from a distant fire could be sighted. A compass bearing on the fire could be transmitted to headquarters by bush telephone. If a fire could be seen from two or more towers, its exact location could be determined through triangulation.

The bush telephone system was used within the park until the early 1970s. The system was put in place with much hard and unending maintenance by the park rangers, particularly Alvin and Aubrey Dunne. The phone system was begun in about 1922; a major expansion took place in 1930. Aubrey recalled extending an existing line. "I can't recall how long it was, but I know we

Park Rangers John Joe Turner, Charlie Brewer and Sam Sunstrum at Basin Depot in 1926. — ALGONQUIN PARK MUSEUM

extended the line because I can recall carrying the wire in. We carried number nine wire rolls [of] 160 pounds . . . roughly a half mile of telephone line and you carried those on your back. This was rugged work, I tell you! . . . Most of the bush telephones were built on trees. . . . You used a pole . . . where no trees existed, or trees were too small to support the telephone wire." Eventually all the ranger cabins and towers in the park were connected.

Aubrey Dunne was also a telephone lineman for the park. He patrolled a vast area with a dog team. "I had dogs, I think, from 1932 or 1933 up until the spring of 1941. When I was living in Whitney and using dog teams to patrol, I can recall leaving Whitney in the morning and going into the park and cross-country down to Basin Depot and being there for supper in the evening, fifty miles. On one occasion . . . 1935 or so . . . [the superintendent] got in touch with me and told me the telephone lines were out. He wanted me to take the dog team to Cache Lake and then endeavour to find out where the trouble was, somewhere west of that. . . . I found the trouble at McCraney, and then I came back down by way of Brûlé Lake and down to Cache. Before I went back to Whitney he thought I should go down to the south park boundary . . . and then follow the park line through to Whitney. Which I did, of course. That meant sleeping in the bush overnight."

The Fairchild used by Superintendent MacDougall for poacher and fire patrol. — ALGONQUIN PARK MUSEUM

Superintendent Frank MacDougall did not bring the first airplane to Algonquin Park. An HS2L flying-boat pusher-type biplane, operated by the Canada Air Board, was located at Whitney for fire patrol in 1922, and at Cache Lake in 1923. At this time, the use of aircraft to detect fire was experimental. In 1924, the Department of Lands and Forests' Ontario Provincial Air Service was formed for fire patrols. By 1931, the HS2L was replaced by a Fairchild, which could be used in summer fire patrols and winter surveillance for poaching and illegal fishing. An airplane hangar was built at Cache Lake. At first, radio communication with the plane was restricted to Morse code; only later was voice transmission possible. In 1938, a larger Stinson Reliant replaced the Fairchild, and the base of operations was moved to its present location at Smoke Lake. A hangar was built in 1939, with the aircrew occupying quarters upstairs.

The hangar provided a maintenance area and shelter for the aircraft. Winter operations required special techniques to combat the cold. According to Joe Holmberg, a technician, before every flight the maintenance crews replenished the engine oil, stored "in pails which were kept on the back of the stove in the shop, between flights. The oil was in a five-gallon pail that sat in a larger pail of water. The aircraft was pushed out onto the railroad ramp and the engine warmed up under a nose-cover tent with a blow pot. Then down the ramp off the platform . . . and onto the

ice . . . and off to flying duty." The pilot and engineer would have snowshoed a packed runway on the lake ice so that the plane would not get stuck in slush. When the plane landed at the hangar, "the winch would pull the airplane back onto the carriage and anchor [it] there. It would be pulled back into the hangar on the carriage, where the hot oil was drained again into the pail and returned to its place on the back of the stove."

With the plane, MacDougall could keep a close watch on the operations of the park. An article in the government periodical *Aski* summed up MacDougall's personal touch: "Man by man he knew many of the people in the small headquarters and on the lonely patrols. He could drop into a clearing in the bush and talk on equal terms with fire fighters and technicians. In fact, he was in and out of more clearings than a swamp rabbit — to see, to learn and to plan."

Having a pilot as superintendent was so successful that when MacDougall became deputy minister of Lands and Forests in 1941, his successors — James Taylor, George Phillips and Yorky Fiskar — were all flyers.

MacDougall helped in the development of the De Havilland Beaver bush plane in the 1940s, through design suggestions and a promise of an order of twenty-five Beavers for the air service. Later the design was modified by the addition of water tanks on the floats. The stored water could be dropped on fires. By 1958, all Beavers and Otters were equipped with the float-type water tanks.

Lookout towers continued to be staffed during the 1950s, though gradually they were phased out. (The last one was abandoned in 1975.) The park continued to be patrolled by the pilots: men such as Ralph Stone, Tom Cooke, George Campbell, Dave Croal and Bill Cram. Rescue flights were flown, interior maintenance and lake survey crews were dropped off and picked up, lakes were stocked with fish. During the mid-1960s, park planes removed garbage recovered from the park interior. Today De Havilland Turbo-Beavers and Turbo-Otters serve the park, assisted by helicopters.

Algonquin, as always, must be protected from some of its visitors. Although no longer called upon to engage in long snowshoe treks or to live in isolated shelter huts, the modern park wardens and conservation officers still patrol along the highway or in the interior — like the rangers of old, ensuring compliance with regulations, educating novice canoeists and sharing with visitors their appreciation of Algonquin Park.

It may be said there are hundreds of lakes scattered through the park in every direction.

JOHN MACOUN, 1903

10

PARK VISITORS

Loggers, rangers and poachers were not the only people in Algonquin Park after 1893. A trickle of visitors, mostly American, came to Algonquin soon after the park was established. George Hayes of Buffalo, a prison commissioner, visited the area to camp and fish as early as 1880. Photographs taken on the Hayes trips of 1896 and 1897 indicate that the gentlemen were accompanied by Ojibwa guides, who were responsible for ensuring their comfort. The tents were heavy canvas over wooden poles. The large view-camera with tripod captured many images of the bearded Mr. Hayes in the bow of his canoe, fishing rod in hand, while his guide manoeuvred the canoe into position below the rapids, a net at the ready. (The speckled trout caught were admirable in both number and size.) Most of the early visitors to the park were men, but of thirty-eight visitors in 1896, five were women.

Another visitor to the area at this time was an in-law of the lumberman J.R. Booth. In 1896, A.W. Fleck bought 5,000 acres (2,023 ha) of land including two islands on the east shore of Rock Lake (not yet inside the park boundary) from the St. Anthony Lumber Company. In 1898, Fleck built a large summer home next to the railway on this land. Later inherited by his daughter, Mrs. Gregor Barclay, the house was occupied until 1953 and dismantled in 1957.

In August 1910, Joseph Adams, an English author, visited the park. His guide on the trip was a park ranger, Mark Robinson, who paddled the canoe and chauffeured Adams to various fishing spots. The men stayed in shelter huts, and Robinson entertained Adams at night with his knowledge of beavers, wolves and other wildlife. The scenes that passed beside the canoe found a place in Adams's *Ten Thousand Miles Through Canada* and may have inspired others to try a canoe trip. "The wealth of beauty into which these waterways lead is probably unsurpassed by anything Canada possesses in forest scenery. The lakes with their wooded slopes and shapely promontories; the islets clad in green from the pale shade of the birch to the deep tint of the pine and balsam; and the restfulness of it all, a broad expanse of water, ruffled only with the gentle breeze that chases rippling waves along its banks, and makes panpipe music amongst its reeds and rushes." Adams maintained that one could only appreciate the park on a camping trip such as his, on which he "wandered out under the stars and again listened to that mysterious negative, the silence of the forest."

Maps had been developed from the township surveys for administrative use. Soon other maps were produced by William Bell and by George Brown, indicating portages and noting lake names, many of which are unchanged on modern canoe-route maps. Certain routes became particularly popular and were designated by colour on some maps. By 1934, as routes became more heavily travelled, it became necessary to develop a system of tourist campsites "consisting of selected locations cleared of ground debris and fitted with tent poles, fire places, tables and latrines." Campsites and portages were identified by wooden signs. A concern that interior users have properly maintained water levels, first noted by Superintendent MacDougall in 1934, led to the rebuilding and maintenance of former logging dams, into the 1960s.

Two humorous books written in the 1940s also helped to raise public interest in canoeing trips. John Robins's award-winning 1944 book *The Incomplete Anglers* was read by more than fishermen. It described the author's canoe trip from Radiant Lake, along the Crow River to Lake Lavieille and south across Dickson and Opeongo lakes. In 1948, Bernard Wickstead wrote *Joe Lavally and the Paleface*, which recounted an Englishman's guided canoe trip north from Canoe Lake to Big Trout Lake. Although guides are still available, since the 1950s and 1960s most people have canoed and camped on their own. Canoe tripping continues to be one of the most popular of Algonquin activities.

There were also longer-term visitors in the park. In his 1886 letter to Thomas Pardee, Alexander Kirkwood had suggested that "seekers for health and pleasure in the summer season may be allowed to lease locations for cottages or tents." The report of the Royal Commission of 1893 made provision for such

George Hayes in camp, 1897. — ALGONQUIN PARK MUSEUM

permanent summer residences, on condition that the land not "be sold or otherwise disposed of for settlement, mining, or other purposes," and that "the title . . . should remain in the hands of the government." Provision was made in the *Algonquin Park Act* of 1893 for "the construction of buildings for ordinary habitation, and such other buildings as may be necessary for the accommodation of visitors or persons resorting to the park as a . . . health or summer resort."

The superintendent's report of 1896 indicates that two parties of visitors were interested in locations suitable to lease. In his 1901 annual report, Superintendent Bartlett commented that soon the requests for summer residence leases would have to be addressed. Shortly thereafter, probably in 1905, Dr. A.J. Pirie purchased two unoccupied lumber company cottages on Canoe Lake as a summer home. Others soon followed, on Cache Lake and Canoe Lake.

In his report of 1912, Superintendent Bartlett recommended that no leases be granted in the north of the park, to preserve that area from development. The government continued to advertise leases. In 1931, newly appointed Superintendent MacDougall suggested a policy intended to "clarify the whole situation, as well as encourage increased leasing." He recommended that the leases be concentrated along the two railways, but not in the interior, thus dividing the park "into regions of residence and wilderness." MacDougall argued that "the railways are the biggest fire hazards, and the cottagers along the railways will help our fire protection." If the administration in Toronto were to "accept this policy, we can furnish our rangers with a list of lakes open to lease, so that they can sell the idea to all suitable tourists who enquire about land." MacDougall's policy was to continue until 1954, when there were approximately 450 leases in the park.

The Royal Commission report of 1892 suggested that "for the convenience of visitors, hotels might, under proper restrictions, be allowed at certain points." Thus, the 1893 legislation provided for commercial leases "where trade and industry necessary for accommodation of persons resorting to the park may be carried on."

One of the first lodges was the Hotel Algonquin, built in 1908 by Tom Merrill, next to the Joe Lake railway station. It was later bought by Mr. and Mrs. Edwin Colson, who operated it until 1943. George Merrydew, and later Gordon Street operated it until 1956. A 1921 railway brochure described the lodge: "The house is built of red pine slabs with the bark on, giving a 'log Inn' effect, and is furnished on the inside in hard wood. There are accommodations for fifty guests and additional accommodations for thirty-five more are afforded in comfortable furnished tents."

Most famous of the lodges was the Highland Inn at Cache Lake, constructed in three stages between 1908 and 1910 by the Canadian Railway News. Following 1928 it was sublet by T.M. Clarke, then after 1938 by Mr. and Mrs. Paget. It dominated the hill behind Algonquin Park Station, near Park Headquarters. The inn being only a stone's throw from the tracks, special rules restricted the use of train whistles so as not to inconvenience the guests. One section of the inn was winterized, and special brochures encouraged winter visits, although at that time of year the lodge likely operated at a loss. The Highland Inn accommodated 150 guests. Visitors could enjoy the well-equipped dining room, writing and reading rooms, and billiard room. For entertainment there was a dance pavilion, bowling green and tennis court. Of course, there were canoes and boats for rental, as well as canoe trip outfitting and guiding services. There was a small grocery store in the basement, and a post office nearby. The inn was dismantled in 1957.

In 1913, Mowat Lodge opened in what had been a boarding house of the Gilmour Company at Canoe Lake. It was run by Shannon and Annie Fraser, who were known for their sociability and good food. The lodge took its name from the village of Mowat, which had grown up beside the lumber mill and railway sidings. The lodge burned down in 1920, was rebuilt on the old mill site by the lake and burned again in 1930.

Mowat Lodge is best known today as artist Tom Thomson's Algonquin base. He first visited the lodge in 1912, and became a regular, either staying in the lodge, camping across the lake and taking a few meals there or guiding for other visitors. Thomson also worked as a fire ranger in the east end of the park.

The Hotel Algonquin in 1922. — ALGONQUIN PARK MUSEUM

One of Algonquin's most famous artists, Tom Thomson, at Cauchon Lake in 1916. — NATIONAL GALLERY OF CANADA

One of the best known of Algonquin's lodges was the Highland Inn at Cache Lake. — ALGONQUIN PARK MUSEUM

There is no doubt that the many attractions of the Park will ere long be eagerly sought out by parties of tourists from all the cities of Ontario.
JAMES WILSON, 1893

It was also from Mowat Lodge that Thomson reportedly set out in July 1917 on the short fishing trip that was to be his last. Many theories have developed over the years to explain the circumstances of his death. Daphne Crombie, a confidante of Annie Fraser's, said Thomson was accidentally killed by Shannon Fraser. Other sources say Thomson was murdered by a person known or unknown to him. The brief coroner's inquest determined that he drowned. The family had the body exhumed from the first burial place at the Canoe Lake cemetery and reburied at Leith, near Owen Sound.

On a hill behind the former site of Mowat Lodge is the Canoe Lake cemetery. Within the fence are the grave markers of James Watson, a mill-hand killed by accident, and Alexander Hayhurst, a young victim of diphtheria. Outside the fence, a grave was dug for Tom Thomson. The passage of time and the discovery in 1956 of a body in Thomson's grave site have added to the mystery surrounding his death. Yet Tom Thomson's significance in Algonquin Park comes not from his death there but from his vivid images of the landscape and the logging industry that so influenced the scenes he painted.

Thomson spent much of his first season in the park in the vicinity of Canoe and Smoke lakes. A 1912 sketch, *Nominigan Point*, depicted the point of land on Smoke Lake selected that spring by the Grand Trunk Railway to be the site for its Camp Nominigan. Fully operational by June of 1913, it was an outpost of the Highland Inn, and a sojourn there was far from roughing it in the bush.

The Bertram cottage on Canoe Lake in the early 1900s.
— ALGONQUIN PARK MUSEUM

Nominigan Camp could be reached by canoe from Canoe Lake Station or by horse-drawn wagon from the Highland Inn along a bush road. A brochure of the time announced "High Altitude — Pure Air — Unspoiled Forest — Beautiful Lakes — Splendid Fishing — Much Wild Game — Hotel and Camp Life."

There were accommodations for sixty guests as well as staff. In the main lodge were four bathrooms and twelve bedrooms on the first and second floors. Each was equipped with yellow porcelain wash bowls and pitchers. Guests could sit on the wide verandah across the front of the lodge or next to the large central fireplace, which warmed both dining room and living room. Meals were prepared on a large wood-burning stove in the kitchen, close to the well-supplied pantry.

The six large guest cabins sat on a small ridge, east of the lodge, staff dining room and ice house. Each comprised a living room with stone fireplace, a bathroom and four bedrooms, two downstairs and two off a balcony at the top of a spiral staircase. Water pressure was maintained by an elevated water tank; waste was disposed of in a septic tank. Lighting was provided by acetylene lamps. The cabins burned down in 1926 and the lodge was sold in 1931 to Garfield and Jesse Northway. It passed to Harry and Adele Ebbs in 1962 and was dismantled in 1977.

Minnesing Camp on Burnt Island Lake was a "sister" lodge, also built by the Grand Trunk Railway in 1913. In 1923, the lease was assigned to Dr. Henry Sherman, who used it for a religious retreat before selling to Manly Sessions in 1947. An early visitor described the 10-mile (16 km) Minnesing Road as so rough with boulders

We have a great many visitors whose sole desire is to breathe our pure air and wander about in the splendid woods of our park.
GEORGE BARTLETT, 1917

Along with Killarney Lodge and Bartlett Lodge, Arowhon Pines Lodge continues to serve park visitors. — EUGENE KATES COLLECTION

Minnesing Camp on Burnt Island Lake was reached by boat or by cart trail. — ALGONQUIN PARK MUSEUM

The sitting room at Minnesing. — ALGONQUIN PARK MUSEUM

as to risk the breakdown of a wagon at any time. One had to decide whether to ride or walk behind the wagon, the latter frequently being preferable.

The lodge itself had an idyllic setting. According to a Grand Trunk Railway pamphlet of 1922: "The cool zephyrs of evening wafted from the lake invoke slumber, invite pleasant dreams and make the dawn a blessing and an inspiration." As at Nominigan, the main lodge was constructed of massive cedar logs. On either side were three cabins described in a 1950s brochure as "ideal for compact groups or families offering all the privacy of individual summer homes. Each has a spacious, two story high living room . . . with a natural stone fireplace and comfortably furnished with splint rockers and arm chairs. The two downstairs bedrooms are served by complete bath. . . . Upstairs are found two more bedrooms, served by a half bath. . . . Each of the six Lodges is separated from its neighbours by forest growth, affording privacy." The Minnesing buildings were returned to the government in 1954 and destroyed in 1957.

Bartlett Lodge on Cache Lake was opened by Alf Bartlett, son of the park superintendent, on the former J.E. Colson cottage site. When the "lodge" started is open to interpretation. Bartlett, like others on the lake, may have run a boarding house for overflow from the Highland Inn, perhaps as early as 1917. His "De'il May Care" cabin may be one of the oldest on the lake. The lodge appears to have opened officially in 1923. Today there is a dining lodge and cabins, reached from the highway by water taxi across a bay of the lake. Although there have been changes through ownership transfer from Bartlett to Charles Daw to Mark Freeman, Bartlett Lodge continues to serve the Cache Lake community and vacationers.

In 1926, Sandy Haggert got a Licence of Occupation for a building originally built by the St. Anthony Lumber Company at Sproule Bay on Lake Opeongo. He opened Opeongo Lodge there in 1928. The lodge was transferred to Joseph Avery in 1936 and burned down in 1957. Since that time, the site has become an outfitting facility leased from the government.

Lake Traverse Camp, on Lake Travers in the eastern section of the park, was opened sometime during the late 1920s. It was described in a 1929 railway pamphlet as a new lodge located "on a wooded knoll [that] affords a charming view of the lake. The large central lodge, which is fully screened comprises dining room and lounge." Sleeping accommodation was tents on platforms and two-person cabins. A 1932 brochure boasted year-round operation and indicated that "at White Partridge Lake, 15 miles distant from the main lodge, there is a well equipped tent camp with central dining room, board floor sleeping tents and

a fine bathing beach . . . . Free wagon transportation is provided from the main lodge to White Partridge Camp." The lease was cancelled in 1949.

Associated with Lake Traverse Camp was Turtle Lodge, built in 1933 by the J.R. Booth Lumber Company. The impressive log structure was in the shape of a turtle (styled after the "bark mark" of the lumber company). Turtle Lodge was eventually bought by a private fishing club. The Ontario government gave permission for the unique structure to be dismantled in 1978, despite its having been designated a "historic zone."

During approximately the same period, Wigwam Lodge operated on Lake Kioshkokwi, near the village of Kiosk. It was described in a 1932 railway pamphlet as offering "real camp life with the rough edges taken off. Surrounding the log cabin lodge and dining room are the cabins and tented sleeping quarters on raised rustic platforms furnished with iron beds and plenty of blankets."

In 1928, Kish-kaduk Lodge was opened at Cedar Lake by Mr. and Mrs. Edwin Thomas. It comprised a main lodge of logs, flanked by comfortably furnished cabins. The lodge was operated until approximately 1975 by Rose Thomas and Jack Wilkinson.

A 1929 Canadian National Railways brochure advertised Camp of the Red Gods, on Tepee Lake. Operated by Elsworth Jeager and Ernest Thompson Seton, it provided "a large central lodge which serves as a dining room, extension library and recreation hall, around which are sleeping cabins of varying sizes to accommodate two persons or groups or families. . . . Educational programs [are] conducted in photography, woodcraft, Indian lore and other subjects." It closed in 1933.

With the building of a park road in 1935, recreational possibilities increased, but Superintendent MacDougall discouraged them. In 1934, he wrote, "Dance halls and all such forms of entertainment can be found at many places elsewhere in Ontario, and it is unnecessary to try and duplicate such forms of entertainment in the park. All such exotic forms of recreation, therefore, should be discouraged, except when they are used in conjunction with summer hotels."

In 1935, Killarney Lodge was opened next to the highway at Lake of Two Rivers by B.W. Moore. It was later run by Elwood Moore and Paul Begrow. The lodge is still operating under the ownership of Eric Miglin.

In 1937, Musclow's Camp at Tea Lake was built and run by Charles Musclow, until 1944, when his sister, Gertie Baskerville, took it over. Guests were accepted into the five cabins until 1970.

Whitefish Lodge at Whitefish Lake was opened in 1939 by Charles Young. In 1945, ownership was transferred to John

Still a popular location, the Portage Store is pictured here in the early days of its operation. — ALGONQUIN PARK MUSEUM

Setting out on a canoe trip from Camp Northway in 1915.
— ALGONQUIN PARK MUSEUM

Connolly, who operated it until 1965, when the property reverted to the government.

Arowhon Pines Lodge was opened in 1942 on Baby Joe Lake by Mrs. Lillian Kates. The large dining lodge, with its central "camboose style" fireplace, is surrounded by many cabins. The lodge, now operated by Eugene Kates, is reached from the highway along the Arowhon Road.

Ralph Bice, famous Algonquin guide and historical writer in his later years, opened Poplar Point, a fishing lodge, at Rain Lake in 1944. According to Mr. Bice, the lodge is "still going strong."

Little is known of two other lodges in the park. In 1949, Glen Donald Lodge was opened on Source Lake by Patrick MacDonald; it closed in 1958. Kingscote Lodge, at Kingscote Lake in the park's "southern panhandle," came within the park boundary in 1961, with annexation of Clyde and Bruton townships. The lodge closed in the late 1980s.

Apart from the lodges, there were also a few stores and restaurants. Molly Cox went to the park for her health in 1900 and stayed to run the rangers' boarding house at Cache Lake. In 1907, she married ranger Edwin Colson. The Colsons operated a store at the head of Canoe Lake from about 1915. In about 1937, shortly after the construction of the park highway, the Portage Store was opened by the Colsons. Today it is an outfitting store and restaurant concession, leased from the government.

Other early stores were far from the modern concessions one finds today along Highway 60 (the Two Rivers and Opeongo stores). A small log store operated at Rock Lake, serving the small community around the railway station. Only a phone booth

marks the spot today. The old-time general store at Brent, an active but small railway community on the shore of Cedar Lake, was run by Gerry McGaughey, who took over the store from a man named Scotty. Generous with canoeists in need of supplies, he also supplied George's Restaurant. George Matise was described by a leaseholder and canoe tripper, Ed Kase, as "a character. He wore this little white apron that was very dirty. . . . He accomplished three things seemingly in one motion: he cooked, he waited on table, he washed dishes all more or less simultaneously. The food was stacked up. There was one price for the meal. . . . You'd go in and say 'I want a dinner.' Almost always when we showed up he would exclaim, terribly surprised, 'Oh, fifteen of you!' Good heavens, I have no food. What can I do?' . . . Then he'd go over to the general store and pick up some food and go back and cook the meal. He'd have a plate with sliced bread, stacked up in two stacks, big jar of jam on the table, a pound of butter, of course the sugar and everything else. There was no limit to the amount you could eat. He just kept bringing it on." George frequently cooked with an oil lamp in one hand so he could see.

Some of the most enthusiastic visitors to Algonquin are the young people who spend summers at youth camps in the park. General activities at the early camps included swimming, canoeing, lifesaving, canoe tripping and regattas. Secondary activities were nature study, arts and crafts and native lore. Central to these activities was a canoe trip, during which campers learned to work and live together under challenging circumstances.

The river flowed without a murmur...
JOSEPH ADAMS, 1912

Campers have played many important roles in the park. During the Second World War, for example, the camps took on portage maintenance and fire protection within defined areas or canoe routes. The Department of Lands and Forests assisted when needed. Open-fronted log shelters were constructed by the camps on certain lakes.

The first and longest-running camp in the park is Northway Lodge on Cache Lake. The camp was established in 1906 by Miss Fanny Case of Rochester, N.Y., who moved it to Algonquin. In 1908, she and a group of girls chose a new site and set up the camp, as described in her *History of Northway Camp*: "The first year of this camp was the greatest year of all, say the campers. . . . It was almost perfect pioneering — no other campers or people about; drinking water was carried laboriously from a spring across the lake; many piles of debris were to be taken care of. . . . The dining room and lodge were large rented tents. The little kitchen was finished the day before camp opened, the roof made so flat by amateur builders that it leaked all summer into the cooks' tea, which they did not mind, being good campers." A boys' camp component, Camp Wendigo, was added in 1965. Today, the campers still live in tents and meals are prepared on the old wood stove.

In 1908, Camp Waubuno for boys was opened on Wabeno Island in Cache Lake, under the direction of G.G. Bowers of Blair Academy, New Jersey. In its brochure, the camp was described as "a village of double roofed waterproof tents high and dry on raised board floors . . . situated on the southern slope of a rocky well-wooded island."

Long Trail Camp, later known as Camp Ahmeek, on Little Joe Lake, opened in 1911 under the directorship of A.W. Field of Columbus Academy, Columbus, Ohio. Accommodation was in tents on raised wooden floors; a central lodge provided shelter for dining and in case of rainy weather. A railway brochure of 1922 suggests that "it is the purpose of those in charge of this camp to develop a spirit of resourcefulness and manly independence by giving each boy a large share of the duties and discipline of the camp." Camp Ahmeek was closed after the 1922 season.

At Camp Waubuno, Cache Lake. — ALGONQUIN PARK MUSEUM

In 1911, Camp Minnewawa was begun at Lake of Two Rivers. It was directed by Prof. W.L. Wise of Bordentown Military Institute, New Jersey. The camp was located where the Two Rivers East Picnic Area is now. In a letter of April 15, 1946, Mrs. J. Cartwright described the camp: "...we had a nice big kitchen and a grand cook stove. Also a large dining room with two long tables and a table each side and a big room ... where all the bedding was kept and under the kitchen was a big cellar and all the cooking utensils and lovely tableware. There was a big boathouse and Mr. and Mrs. Wise had a nice cabin of their own. The summer I was there Mr. Wise had 35 boys all from the school he taught in. ... Most of the boys that came, their parents went abroad in the summer." Camp letterhead of 1917 portrays a central log building in front of roughly a dozen tents. The camp was closed about 1930.

In 1914, Camp Pathfinder was opened on an island in Source Lake, by Herman Norton of Rochester, New York. The camp was styled as a wood-craft camp in real camping country. Like those at other camps, the first campers stayed in tents. The camp is still operating.

Taylor Statten of Camp Ahmek, Canoe Lake, first came to Algonquin Park in 1912 on a canoe trip. He and his wife, Ethel, so enjoyed the Canoe Lake area that they purchased a lease on Little Wapomeo Island in 1913, building their cottage three years later. Statten believed that a better world could be created through young men's experience of the camping movement. In 1917, he invited camping specialists to Little Wapomeo Island. A result was the establishment of the Camp Tuxis leadership camp, held on Canoe Lake in 1920 and 1921. One hundred and forty leadership candidates attended the first camp to learn from specialists in wildlife and wood-lore, including the goose specialist Jack Miner and the local naturalist and park ranger Mark Robinson.

In 1921, Statten's Camp Ahmek was opened on the beach where Camp Tuxis had been held. Over the years the beach was cleared of debris and the camp grew. An early camp brochure states, "The camp ... circles a bay with a half a mile of sand beach. Away from tourists, yet with a daily delivery of milk and produce, enjoying the freedom of isolation, yet the centre of canoe trips; with its altitude and immunity from hay fever, the site is admirably fitted as a summer home for boys."

The original Camp Ahmek, Canoe Lake. — ALGONQUIN PARK MUSEUM

Camp Tanamakoon girls on a canoe trip, Narrowbug Lake, c. 1948.
— ALGONQUIN PARK MUSEUM

In 1922, Mrs. Statten opened Camp Wapomeo for girls on Little Wapomeo Island. By 1927, it had grown so large that the senior girls moved to Wapomeo Island; the rest of the camp moved to the island in 1931. Since Taylor Statten's death in 1956 the camps have been managed by members of the family.

There also appears to have been a Camp Opeongo, during the 1920s, run by a Colonel James. A park ranger on Opeongo Lake told Ron Perry, an early instructor at Camp Ahmek, that after the First World War an English army officer established a boys' camp at Lake Opeongo. Although it was planned for two hundred campers, only a few showed up and the location was abandoned after the first summer. Had the camp continued, getting there would have been a challenge. A 1924 railway map shows Camp Opeongo at the site of the former Dennison farm. Trains would stop at the head of Whitefish Lake; from there campers would have to canoe and portage many kilometres to the camp.

An outpost of Glen Bernard Camp for girls in Sundridge started in 1924, at North Tea Lake. It operated for at least eight years, but little more is known about it.

In 1925, Camp Tanamakoon for girls was begun at White (Tanamakoon) Lake, near Park Headquarters, by Mary G. Hamilton. The site was relatively isolated but close enough to the Highland Inn for parents to stay there. As well, the location would avoid the difficulties others had encountered getting supplies to their facilities. The main building contained a kitchen, dining room and recreation room. The thirty-five campers, two counsellors and director stayed in tents. Today the camp is considerably bigger, with many facilities.

Camp Arowhon was established in 1934 at the former site of Camp of the Red Gods, on Tepee Lake, by Mrs. Lillian Kates. It was the park's first co-educational camp, and remains so.

Last of the camps still operating in the park is Camp Tamakwa. Founded in 1937 by Lou Handler of Detroit, Michigan, the camp is located on the north shore of Tea Lake.

A few camps lasted only a short time and little is known about them. In 1946, J. McKechnie opened Forest Bay Boys' Camp, which operated on Galeairy Lake for a few years. Douglas Gardner, a Toronto teacher, opened Camp Douglas on Whitefish Lake in 1951. It closed about 1958.

The last new camp in the park, on the site of Camp Douglas, opened as a result of a 1973 government decision to continue and expand summer camps in the park. Opened in 1974, the Algonquin Experience Youth Camp was operated by the YMCA. A camp brochure described the camp as "a resident camping experience in Algonquin Park for young people in Ontario who would enjoy such an experience, but do not have access to the opportunity." The camp closed about 1982.

Another organized group of young people has played an important role in Algonquin. In 1937, under Superintendent Frank MacDougall, thirty young men of his Dominion-Provincial Youth Training Plan were stationed in buildings used for construction of the airfield, two years earlier, at Lake of Two Rivers. They were paid to learn fire-fighting techniques, telephone line installation, timber cruising and other bush skills, as well as to clear brush for campsites, particularly in the new campground on the lake. (This program was the precursor of the Junior Rangers, now the Ontario Rangers.)

Purple-fringed orchis

Cardinal flower

Blue flag iris

Pink moccasin flower

Campers at Lake of Two Rivers campground during the Second World War. — ALGONQUIN PARK MUSEUM

Roadside camping in Algonquin Park developed with the highway and brought a new type of visitor. Like the clearing of the Two Rivers airfield, Highway 60 was constructed as a result of grants made by the federal government to help relieve unemployment during the Depression. MacDougall foresaw problems of logistics that would need prompt solutions. "Facilities for overnight motorists are necessary and . . . provision must be made for transient campers by the construction of two camp-sites at least, so that the areas where cottagers are will not be congested with over-night campers. These sites will need quite a lot of work to make room for tent platforms, docks, latrines, kitchens, fireplaces, drinking water supplies, and all the other accessories that will be needed at a place where motorists stop."

In 1935, small campsites, which were later expanded, opened at Lake of Two Rivers, Tea Lake and Tea Lake Dam. Rudy Humber and his wife visited Lake of Two Rivers the year the road was completed. "The park was beautiful. Rather primitive but beautiful. We came in the park in 1935 with a very small tent.

Found a group of wonderful people who liked nature as we did. We had a great time and the next year we copied our friends in the park and brought a large tent, gasoline stove, sleeping bags, etc., etc. The roads were very bad. Very dusty, although there was not much traffic in those days. . . . Most of the folks at the campsite were professional people, doctors, clergymen, etc."

Now that passenger trains are gone, Algonquin can only be reached by road. There are campsites at Tea Lake, Pog Lake, Mew Lake, Lake of Two Rivers, Canisbay Lake, Rock Lake, Coon Lake, Kearney Lake and at some of the access points to the park. More than 1,600 interior campsites have been designated along the canoe routes and hiking trails in the interior. The park continues to be used by a large number of visitors, at campsites, lodges, summer camps, cottages and in the interior.

From its beginning, recreational uses and the continued utilization of the forests for lumber had a significant effect on the park's lakes, forests and wildlife. How much? In what way? These were questions in need of answers.

The Commissioner of Crown Lands who establishes Algonkin Forest and Park raises a monument that will not crumble nor decay...
ALEXANDER KIRKWOOD, 1886

11

LOOKING FOR ANSWERS

One of the aims of the 1893 Royal Commission on the proposed Algonquin Park was "to provide a field for experiments in and practice of systematic forestry upon a limited scale." Another was to maintain a reservoir of animals. During the first hundred years of its history, systematic research and subsequent planning played an important role in determining the extent and nature of Algonquin Park resource use.

The first scientist to visit Algonquin Park was John Macoun, assistant director and naturalist of the Geological Survey of Canada. From May to August 1900, Macoun travelled widely through the park, collecting and/or recording many plant specimens to fill in gaps in the knowledge of Central Ontario botany. Macoun's travels were mostly in the western section of the current park. From specimen labels and his report we know that he travelled to Lake Opeongo on the east, Rain Lake on the west and the Petawawa River to the north. He also travelled the well-frequented route through Big Trout and the Otterslides to Catfish and Cedar lakes. Macoun's visit to the park took place before the extensive hardwood logging of the 1920s and before the pine forests recovered from their logging. Thirty-one of the species Macoun collected or reported are not found in the park today.

Macoun and his assistant, William Spreadborough, also collected information on birds, fish, reptiles and insects, and made general observations about the forests and the impact of people on it.

The forest within the park is still largely in a state of nature, except that the white pine has been cut out more or less completely everywhere. . . . The value of the forest as a covering for the soil and as a retainer of moisture cannot be over-estimated. . . . The effects of the passage of the railway and the cutting of lumber roads through the park, were well illustrated by the introduction of species of plants that are found as weeds in the open spaces and around dwellings. These have been followed by a few species of birds and a number of butterflies, so that every year greater changes will be observed. . . .

The early superintendents were much interested in "improving" the park by the introduction of new species. As the area had been set aside as a game preserve, they wished to increase the species of animals and birds.

In 1894 and 1895, Peter Thomson made an unsuccessful attempt to establish wild rice, sure that it would attract more waterfowl to the park. Thomson also proposed a systematic re-establishment of white pine. Seed sent from Toronto was planted experimentally to determine the best time to plant. Superintendents Thomson and John Simpson also planted half a bushel of acorns, some horse-chestnuts, eight Lombardy poplars, and various fruit trees and currant bushes to supplement the vegetable garden at headquarters. Most of the trees did not survive.

Simpson noted the absence of bass in the lakes, and suggested they be stocked. George Bartlett reported in 1899 that "during the past season some 500 very fine black bass, from one to four pounds in weight were brought from Parry Sound and put into Cache, White and Source Lakes."

The introduction was quite successful and changed the nature of the park's fisheries, as predicted by Macoun: "When the lakes have been stocked with food fishes, the denizens of both land and water will change so much that in twenty years hence the present conditions will not be recognizable." Bass had spread through the Madawaska River, 50 miles (80 km) east of the park, by 1906, according to the superintendent's reports. The success of the bass led to suggestions that other species, including rainbow trout and walleye, also be stocked.

Thomson and Simpson also called for the introduction of prairie chicken and rocky mountain grouse. Superintendent Bartlett experimented with caged pheasant, but decided they would not survive in the wild. Instead he introduced fifty-five capercaillie, a large European grouse, but these succeeded only briefly.

In 1896, Superintendent Simpson proposed the introduction of caribou to the park. This was never carried out, though there

Raccoon

for the greater comfort of visitors. In 1932, he had reported on efforts to reduce mosquitoes and blackflies around the Highland Inn and Park Headquarters: "110 gallons of Phinotas Oil were put in the running streams near Cache Lake and effectively killed blackfly larvae wherever the oil was used. . . . No information is available on control of sand flies and very little is known about them. Future experiments should be carried on to determine something about the habits of this insect."

In 1935, MacDougall invited Dr. W.J.K. Harkness, director of the Ontario Fisheries Research Laboratory, to set up in Algonquin Park. Harkness accepted. The first year research was carried out at Cache Lake. During 1936, the Fisheries Research Laboratory at Opeongo Lake was established. (It is now called the Harkness Laboratory of Fisheries Research.) The staff had temporary quarters at Opeongo Lodge until a log structure was built for them. In 1937 and 1938, some staff lived at the abandoned road-construction camp located on the current site of the Costello Lake picnic area. Facilities for all the staff were complete at Opeongo by 1940.

Early and long-term studies were undertaken in basic research and management techniques. A creel census — a tally of statistics on fish caught — was begun in 1936 on Lake Opeongo and later extended to other lakes. It revealed that the annual production of fish in Algonquin lakes was less than 2 pounds per acre (0.4 kg/ha) and that lake rates varied widely. Researchers studied all aspects of aquatic biology. Studies were conducted to better understand the life cycle, food requirements, growth rates, spawning requirements and behaviour of speckled trout, lake trout, and their hybrid, the splake, which was introduced to Algonquin waters in 1954.

During 1944 and 1945, experiments on the use of DDT pesticide were carried out in Algonquin Park. In one study, the substance we now know to be environmentally hazardous was sprayed directly into Brewer and Costello creeks and on Costello Lake; and the considerable numbers and species of insects and fish killed were tallied. The insecticide was also sprayed on forest plots to determine its effects on spruce budworm.

Although most of the fisheries work was done in spring, summer and autumn, Nick Martin, a later director of the lab, recalled research work during the winter of 1950–51: "We were in a log building and it was warm. My wife and I stayed there. . . . We kept an ice hole open in the lake for water. . . . We used to go about our business every day . . . doing a lot of work on lake trout during the winter. Things like food habits and hatching. . . . We were busy, but we didn't get much done. It might take you an hour or two to get the blasted truck down [the road] to the lake."

were caribou not far distant, reported by Bartlett to have been sighted in the park in 1905. However, ten elk were released in January 1935. For a while they seemed to be thriving, but for reasons then unexplained they died out by 1949.

Highway 60 was a stimulus to major research, both by raising concerns about access and by making access easier for researchers. The Ontario Federation of Anglers claimed that "the primary reason for setting up the park was to provide a fish and game sanctuary" yet the road would "result in depletion of wildlife."

Superintendent MacDougall recognized that the road would create a significant increase in fishing pressure on park lakes, and called for a systematic study of the fisheries: "It is hoped that the Park will sometime have within its boundaries a fish laboratory where long-term scientific studies of fish life in general can be carried on." His 1934 report noted that some areas were being heavily fished and called for research before any decisions to restock fish.

One cannot help thinking that MacDougall also took into consideration the tendency to manipulate the park environment

Common loon

Life at the lab was not all serious. Nick Martin remembered a prank the lab staff played on George Holmberg, a ranger, in the early 1950s. "George didn't have much education, so he had a real thing about people who did. One of the things that used to infuriate George was white lab coats and what they stood for." One day when there were many staff and students around, all the lab coats that could be found were rounded up and George's pointer boat was loaded up with researchers in white, "like a bunch of Vikings . . . one guy up in the front with a big pole." George "came out and there was this pointer, which we didn't have permission to have, and all of these white lab coats. Well, he was just going to arrest the whole lot of us. He was furious. That was just too many lab coats at one time."

In his annual report of 1932, MacDougall reported that animal population periodicity studies were being done in the park by staff of the Royal Ontario Museum. In 1937, Duncan MacLulich was involved in work on varying hares. C.H.D. Clarke was doing ruffed grouse research at Brûlé Lake. Duncan MacLulich was later hired by MacDougall to act as a park biologist. (MacDougall couldn't hire him in that capacity, so he was hired as a senior ranger assigned to headquarters.) He published a monograph on birds found in the park, and conducted studies on beaver, mouse and deer populations. He also was influential in the preservation of the Big Crow Lake stand of white pine in 1939.

In 1944, Clarke was involved in the setting up of the Wildlife Research Area around Lake Sasajewun, up a logging road running north from the abandoned sawmill site and airfield at Lake of Two Rivers. During the first two years, the research staff stayed in the old mill bunkhouses, while accommodation was built in the research area and a grid system was laid out to facilitate statistical work on plants and small mammals.

Dr. David Fowle speculated on the role of J.R. Dymond, director of the Royal Ontario Museum, in establishing the Wildlife Research Area: "My impression is that he probably was influential in encouraging Frank MacDougall to establish a wildlife operation in the park that would be a complement to the fisheries work which Dymond had been very much involved in in previous years. The idea was to establish an area, something like thirty square miles, which would be designated and cut off from other uses like canoe trips and logging in order that long-term ecological studies could be done without fear of them being disturbed by anything else."

Setting out vegetation plots at the Wildlife Research Area in the late 1940s. — ALGONQUIN PARK MUSEUM

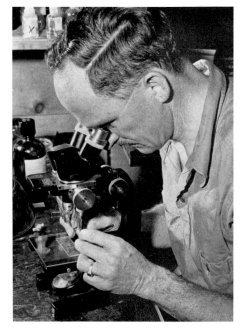

Much of Algonquin's research has been done in the laboratory. Here Murray Fallis studies parasites.
— ALGONQUIN PARK MUSEUM

In the early years, conducting research at the Wildlife Station was not easy. Dr. Murray Fallis recalled "living in tents with the usual wet season you find in June in Algonquin Park and trying to look through microscopes which would fog up when it was cold." Fallis was particularly interested in parasites in grouse and other birds; the parasites were transmitted by blackflies and midges. Techniques used on blackflies by Dr. Fallis and Dr. D.M. Davies at the Wildlife Research Station became known worldwide. "We were asked to go to Africa to study the behaviour of the flies, which carry a disease to twenty million people in Africa. It was because of these basic studies of blackflies in Northern Ontario that they wanted to make use of the information and techniques to study these things of medical importance in Africa."

Dr. Roy Anderson was also interested in parasites, but in larger wildlife. His pioneering work on moose and deer parasites was carried out at the Wildlife Research Station between 1958 and 1964. He was able to determine that when moose and white-tailed deer shared a common range, they also shared a parasite, which was fatal to the moose but harmless to the deer. Anderson discovered that a brain worm was passed from the droppings of deer to snails that fed on the droppings. The infected snails climbed up vegetation, where they were eaten by other deer or moose. Inside the stomach, the worms moved to and up the spinal cord. In moose this resulted in paralysis and eventual death. The brain worm has been found to have a similar effect on elk, which may explain why their introduction to Algonquin failed earlier in the century. Today white-tailed deer numbers are low in Algonquin Park; consequently, the moose population is very successful.

It was in Algonquin Park that much pioneering work on wolves was done — and continues. The need for wolf research was recognized in MacDougall's 1934 report: "Until we know better the relationship between deer and wolves over large areas, it would be illogical to attempt extermination of the wolf." Yet for many years park rangers continued in their efforts to eliminate the wolf.

In 1958, Dr. Douglas Pimlott joined a program of research, co-ordinated by John Shannon, to identify the wolf-pack territories in Algonquin Park. The researchers arranged for an end to the wolf control program in the park in 1959. The research program continued until 1965, when the results were written up for publication.

Puffball (lycoperdom umbrinum)

Polyphemus moth

One of the most interesting aspects of the wolf research involved population-study techniques. In winter, wolves could be easily spotted from a plane but were hidden by even thin summer foliage. It was suggested that the researchers try using tape recordings of wolf howls to elicit responses and thus locate packs. Pimlott contracted William Gunn, sound recordist and former director of the Wildlife Research Station, to record captive wolves. "That summer, 1959, I then hired sound equipment from a company in Toronto . . . with huge horns, amplifiers and tape recorder. So we couldn't do anything with them but carry them around in the back of a truck." The researchers then tried another approach. Pimlott knew that the captive wolves would respond to human imitations of wolf howls. He had some of his students try to get non-captive wolves to respond — and it worked. The technique became pivotal to later research studies on wolf communication and to long-term studies on particular packs, much of which took place near the Wildlife Research Area.

Research is still going on at the Wildlife Research Station, although the area is no longer restricted to travel. Studies on subjects from mice to moose and beaver to bear have benefited from the large block of wildlife habitat available over a long period of time in the park.

Algonquin was also used for forestry study. The University of Toronto regularly held its field camps in the Achray area during the 1920s. In 1949, the Petawawa Management Unit was established in the northeastern section of the park as a model for timber harvest. Soon the entire park was divided into similar management units.

During the late 1940s, it was noticed that throughout Ontario there was little regeneration of the yellow birch, yet much of the forest industry involved yellow birch products. Donald Burton participated in the search for a site for hardwood-forest research. The main criterion was simple: they needed a mature hardwood forest that was not being cut. The search continued on during 1949 and 1950 and a research site was eventually established in Algonquin Park, "which was really the last place we were going because we didn't want to get too involved with the park problems. Although the park problems in those days were rather simple, you didn't have to be a genius to know they were going to get complicated in the future." In 1950, the 2,400-acre (971 ha) Swan Lake Forest Research Area was established in a mature hardwood stand west of Smoke Lake. A road was constructed to the field station in 1952, and a small headquarters building was established. The research focused particularly on the sugar maple and regeneration of yellow birch.

The work on birch research involved setting out hundreds of small plots in the forest and staking out all birch seedlings within the plots. It was discovered that yellow birch sprouted, but survived only where the litter of leaves was not too thick to let the young plant through. Where there was little leaf litter and the seedlings grew, deer preferred to browse on them. The researchers could prove that the deer were limiting birch regeneration as well as that of many other species of tree, such as white birch and cherry. Studies were also undertaken to determine the effects of prescribed burns on maple and birch regeneration.

In 1959, land was set aside near Lake Travers for a 150 foot (46 m) radio telescope. Studies were made from the site of the sun, distant stars and galaxies. Closure of the facility was announced in 1986, though some projects continue there.

No overview of research in Algonquin Park can ignore the pioneering historical work of Audrey Saunders, author of *Algonquin Story*. In 1944, shortly after the park's fiftieth anniversary, she was commissioned by the government to write about the people of Algonquin Park. She had just completed a master's degree in which she had used oral history, and this method served her well. "There was an urgency to this job because the Colsons were very elderly. They were living in the park and [the government] wanted me to go up and talk to them in April. . . . They made arrangements for me to get in and out. I went partly by dog sleigh."

Saunders incorporated information from park newsletters and files, but it was the interviews of the people that made her work so valuable. "What I did was see if I could somehow or other place these people in the context of the park. . . . You talk to key people and you ask them the questions that you want. Of course part of the problem was I kept hitting . . . people who didn't read or write. . . . They're suspicious if they see you writing things. So I would use just very small notebooks that I could tear the pages out of, and when they gave me some information I would say, 'Now that's very interesting, do you mind if I get that down?' When they said no, then I'd keep on writing . . . not in any kind of script, but in note form." Saunders's notes are still a treasured resource to the student of Algonquin Park history.

From time to time the research staff have found it necessary or useful to explain their work to park visitors. What began as casual explanations gradually became more organized, culminating in the development of the Algonquin Park Interpretive program, which now operates out of the Visitor Centre overlooking Sunday Creek, on Highway 60. Duncan MacLulich recalled setting out nature-trail labels on the trees on

Interpreter Dick Ussher uses museum specimens to teach a 1951 group of Tanamakoon campers.

— ALGONQUIN PARK MUSEUM

the Canisbay Lake portage in about 1938, and J.R. Dymond used to teach about wildlife during meetings of the Smoke Lake Nature Club in 1942. In 1937, Superintendent Frank MacDougall suggested the Royal Ontario Museum set up a museum in the park. A shortage of funds and personnel during the Depression delayed its establishment until many years later, in 1953.

In 1944, at the request of the Department of Lands and Forests, J.R. Dymond held fifteen public nature walks and made five visits to children's camps. Years later, John Speakman — the Interpretive Program's first seasonal naturalist, in 1945, who also worked at the Wildlife Research Station — remembered J.R. Dymond: "He was marvellous. Just looking at an old rotten pine stump would start him off on the turnover of trees and the decay and the rotting and so on, the development of humus. And he was very good on ferns and amphibians and . . . he'd extol the virtue of the bogs. . . . He just had a natural gift for telling stories."

In 1946, a tent museum was erected at Cache Lake and kept open for fifty-four days during the summer season. The tent museum operated for three summers. A permanent Algonquin Park Museum was erected at Found Lake in 1953; attendance reached 52,000 that season. The museum and the ever-popular evening talks, conducted walks and labelled trails provided entertainment and education for the park visitors. The program has had many changes: the Pioneer Logging Exhibit was added in 1959, the *Raven* began publication in 1960, the first public wolf howl took place in 1963, the museum exhibits were redesigned in 1964, and trail guides and other publications have been co-published with the Friends of Algonquin. Since 1953, the program has been directed by Al Helmsley, Grant Tayler, Bill Calvert, Ron Tozer and Dan Strickland, with assistance from more than one hundred seasonal naturalists and additional support staff.

The Algonquin Logging Museum (opened in 1992), the Algonquin Park Visitor Centre (opened in 1993) and continued research will aid future naturalist staff in bringing to the visitors some of Algonquin's answers.

A perpendicular cliff rears its head for at least one hundred feet skyward, its top crowned with majestic red and white pine.
JAMES DICKSON, 1886

100

12

A Master Plan

Since the early days of the park, access has been getting easier for the visitor. The early tote roads were replaced by the railroads, which in turn were succeeded by a gravel road and then a paved highway. Guided excursions for the wealthy gave way to simpler camping in the interior or in roadside campgrounds, a vacation that was financially possible for just about anyone. This increase in park use resulted in more pressure on park resources and potential conflict among groups with different interests. It was soon evident that planned management was needed.

Superintendent Frank MacDougall had considered areas of potential conflict. In 1935, he described some administrative problems he faced in the park: "It would be easy to maintain the area for scenic purposes only. But when there is added to it the further necessity of permitting logging, the problem is complicated. As each of the ends to be attained is in some respects divergent, if not antagonistic to others, these clashes appear at every turn."

The theme was continued in an article on Multiple Land Use, in which MacDougall explained some of his approaches to management. He wrote:

> A use conflict arises in an area where logging and recreation are two of the ideals. The park area was logged long before there was any park. The increasing use of the area for recreation has intensified the antagonism between the proponents of logging and the users of the forest for recreation. The solution has been to modify logging by . . . removal of shorelines from cutting rights . . . [and] by writing into all renewals or new contracts clauses that will lead to the management of these forests more in keeping with the changing conditions.

In 1930, prior to MacDougall's appointment as superintendent, a shoreline reservation had been put in place around Cache Lake — where headquarters and the Highland Inn were located. By 1939, MacDougall had extended the concept of reservations and multiple use to the park interior:

The chief needs of recreation are good shorelines. In the past five years reservations of shorelines have been made on 39 major lakes, on numerous small lakes, on all the park highway and on a number of the important portages. The logger who purchased the timber pays an annual rental for the land and an annual fire tax for fire ranging and has co-operated in helping the Department solve the difficulties which arise from the attempt to use each piece of land for many conflicting uses. Multiple land use is a new desire of conservationists. Algonquin Park is one of the few areas in North America where land is so being used.

By the late 1940s, other uses of park lands were being made, and questioned. Between 1947 and 1950, a wide corridor running roughly north-south through the middle of the park was cleared of trees during construction of Ontario Hydro's transmission line to carry electrical power from the Ottawa River to Southern Ontario. In the early 1950s, there was increasing demand for leases for private cottages and camps, and requests to provide services for those already in place. Superintendent George Phillips feared businessmen would turn the park into a "honky-tonk of dance halls and hot-dog stands."

Recognizing that people pressures on the park were building, the government prepared a White Paper in 1954. It suggested that more attention be paid to the orderly development of renewable resources in Ontario, called for a review of "present policies of land disposal within Provincial Parks," and recommended further planning. It also endorsed a policy "to provide for the restoration of established Provincial Parks as near as possible to their natural state for the benefit, enjoyment and advantage of the people of Ontario." As inadequate planning had resulted in insufficient recreational facilities in Southern Ontario, something had to be done soon or all future opportunities would be lost to expanding urbanization.

One target of the new policy was the cottage leases. Prior to 1953, government policy had encouraged leasing. MacDougall had once argued that since the land desirable for leasing was of

In the 1940s, trucks began to replace horse-drawn sleighs.
— ALGONQUIN PARK MUSEUM

little use for forestry, "as a solution of idle land use, it is one of the best investments the state can make." However, in June 1954, the provincial cabinet decided to reduce, over the long term, the approximately 450 commercial and private leases in Algonquin Park, which were mostly near the highway. A freeze was placed on new leases for private cottages, children's camps and lodges. Existing leases would be permitted to run to term plus twenty-one years.

In 1956, some of the lodges, such as the Hotel Algonquin and the Highland Inn, were purchased by the government and dismantled the following year. Other leases were bought up as the occupants decided to sell. Between 1956 and 1961, public campgrounds were increased or expanded. Edwin Colson's Portage Store at Canoe Lake was purchased by the government and a refreshment store was opened at Lake of Two Rivers Campground. (These were to be operated on a concession basis.)

Since more people were visiting the park, this led to conflict between interest groups. As access to the park became easier, so did the loggers' ability to cut and haul year-round. By the 1950s, horses and manpower had been replaced by mechanized trucks, skidders and loaders. The river drive gave way to transportation by rail and then by truck. Primitive roads had been constructed for getting supplies to the shanties and timbers to the lakes, but the modern roads were usable year-round, more durable and returned to forest less quickly. As cross-cut saws were replaced by two-man chain saws and then one-man chain saws, the sound of internal combustion engines made park visitors aware of industry that had been a part of the park for a hundred years. Park users could hear the sound of trucks in the distance; see roads where they crossed portages; were wakened from their holiday sleep-in by the intrusion of someone's early start to a long day at a chain saw. For urban-based visitors, the perception of Algonquin Park as wilderness was destroyed.

George B. Priddle, in researching for a master's thesis, had asked park interior users to describe their perception of wilderness and what factors interfered with it. The research was discussed at a 1964 Department of Lands and Forests meeting, which concluded:

> There has to be distance between developed recreational resources, highways, and the "Wilderness." Too many people, garbage, motorboats, and buildings are real interruptions to the "Wilderness". . . . From this knowledge positive steps can be taken to increase the carrying capacity of the Wilderness by dispersing the use, increasing the level of maintenance, outlawing motorboats and stopping the development of public access roads that penetrate deep into the interior of the park.

Technology comes to the woods, with a 1940s chainsaw developed to cut hardwoods. — ALGONQUIN PARK MUSEUM

A government report on planning in the early 1960s noted the number of park users was increasing dramatically:

> There is every indication that this pressure threatens the destruction of the very environment which is the attraction. Since 1958, for example, the numbers of park visitors have increased from 150,000 to almost one-half million; the number of campers using campgrounds accessible by road have [sic] almost doubled to this season's figure of 77,000; the canoe-trippers who travel the interior waterways have tripled their numbers from 10,000 to 32,000. Virtually all areas suitable for campground development . . . are now in the process of becoming overcrowded.

The report called for Natural Zones, Wilderness Zones and Multiple Use Zones.

Work on a Master Plan for Algonquin Park began officially in 1966, under Superintendent T.W. Hueston. A meeting was held in October to which Lands and Forests representatives from Pembroke, Lindsay and Parry Sound districts, as well as head office staff from Research, Fish and Wildlife, Timber, and Parks Branch were invited. Hueston gathered material on the park environment, history and operations, user statistics for all parks and the findings of camper surveys carried out in 1966. Projections suggested that 1967 use would almost double by 1975.

In March 1967, Abbott Conway expressed concern to a legislative committee on natural resources, wildlife and mining about the loss of wilderness that was apparent in Algonquin Park. He became one of the founders of the Algonquin Wildlands League, which held its inaugural meeting in Huntsville in June 1968. The league called on the Ontario Department of Lands and Forests to curtail increasing commercial logging operations and road construction in the interior of the park and to set aside a large part of Algonquin Park as a primitive area, in which canoeists could enjoy a wilderness experience. Other concerns included the rapid rise of mechanized transport and increased noise, air and water pollution. Local communities suggested that the Algonquin Wildlands League and naturalist groups were selfishly undermining the livelihood of the small towns that depended on the lumber industry.

Hard frost last night. Up at half past six this morning. Sun shining bright. Every appearance of a fine day.
STEPHEN WATERS, 1893

Despite the publicity of the park being logged, as if it were a new event, people continued to visit along Highway 60 in even greater numbers. On some weekends in the summer, capacity in the campgrounds was exceeded, specifically in the form of overflow camping spaces on the Lake of Two Rivers airfield. The effect of the overflow eventually became noticeable. In 1968, routine sampling of the drinking water at a cottage on Lake of Two Rivers indicated possible coliform pollution. Systematic sampling by the Leaseholder Association proved there was cause for concern.

The following summer the problem recurred, as reported in the Toronto *Telegram*: "More than 10,000 campers piled into the park's 1,400 designated campsites during the long August Holiday Weekend. . . . Lands and Forests officials were aware that the Lake of Two Rivers was nearing the dangerous pollution stage several weeks before the August holiday." Despite department reassurance that a health hazard was remote, signs were posted in late summer to indicate Lake of Two Rivers was closed for swimming. Plans for a "proposed campground south of Lake of Two Rivers" — on which some road construction had already begun — were abandoned, Superintendent Hueston wrote, "because we haven't been able to gauge the impact on the watershed which already contains most of the car campgrounds."

There were problems in the interior of the park as well. An increased number of canoeists resulted in severe pressure on campsites and portages along popular routes. The garbage left by so many travellers created a problem at frequently used campsites. By the late 1960s, garbage removal cost close to $100,000 a year. Campers were being encouraged to bring non-burnable garbage out of the interior with them and charges for non-compliance were being contemplated.

In 1968, the Ontario government released a Provisional Master Plan on Algonquin Park, which called for the establishment of activity zones within the park: multiple-use zones, in which logging activity would be continued; recreation zones, bordering Highway 60; and two wilderness zones. During public hearings held in November 1968, at Toronto, Pembroke and Huntsville, it rapidly became apparent that most people had been unaware that extensive logging was carried out in Algonquin Park.

Most submissions fell into four groups. Members of the forest industry wanted to protect their long-term leases to cut specific areas and ensure year-round employment, to attract the best employees to their operations. Local residents were concerned about the economic impact of reducing timber-harvesting areas. The Federation of Ontario Naturalists and Algonquin Wildlands League called for larger wilderness zones or a primitive zone;

The experience of older countries has everywhere shown that the wholesale and indiscriminate slaughter of forests brings a host of evils in its train.
ROYAL COMMISSION, 1893

Chipmunk

Calopogon orchid

Logging continues to be a keystone in the regional economy. — ALGONQUIN PARK MUSEUM

no-cut reservations along shorelines and portages; restricted use of outboard motors; and a moratorium on the use of mechanized logging equipment from June 1 to September 30. Angling associations argued against restrictions on fishing in the park and the use of outboard motors. Additionally, leaseholders of cottages, lodges and children's camps expressed concern about their status in the park.

Given the extreme reactions to the Provisional Master Plan, the government decided further public and departmental discussion was needed. In December 1968, the government established a Task Force on Algonquin Park, within the Department of Lands and Forests. Its task was to gather information about the park that would form the basis for recommendations for its management. Much of our detailed knowledge of the natural history of the park came as a result of the extensive inventory of forest habitats taken in order to recommend natural areas worthy of preservation in the zone system. The history of the park and economic conditions in the area surrounding the park were also studied. The task force developed interim guidelines for management to be put in effect until the release of the final Master Plan.

The Algonquin Park Advisory Committee was formed in September 1969 to advise the government on delicate policy decisions. Headed by former premier Leslie Frost, the committee included representatives of the interest groups that had expressed concern about the Provisional Master Plan: six local members of the Ontario Legislature, the mayor of Huntsville, the Federation of Anglers and Hunters, the Ontario Forest Industries Association, the National and Provincial Parks Association, the Federation of Ontario Naturalists, the Conservation Council of Ontario, the Ontario Camping Association, the Smoke Lake Leaseholders' Association and the Algonquin Wildlands League. The committee became familiar with a vast amount of information, presented in a very short time. They visited logging operations and attended lectures examining the issues behind many people's concerns.

In 1973, the Ontario government announced a set of policy decisions based on the recommendations of the Advisory Committee. Leo Bernier, minister of the newly formed Ministry of Natural Resources, announced that the government had firmly decided that Algonquin would not be a single-purpose park. Logging would not be excluded; however, the twenty-four licences held by the logging companies would be cancelled. In their place a Crown Corporation, the Algonquin Forestry Authority, would harvest the timber in Algonquin.

While it lay within our power we have set apart over a million acres of the public domain, and dedicated it to the use and enjoyment not only of ourselves but of the future inhabitants of Ontario.

T.W. GIBSON, 1896

The minister said that the park should continue to be "an average man's wilderness." Cottage and commercial leases, with the exception of children's camps, would continue to be phased out. Lodge leases would be given a common expiry date of 1996. The use of outboard motors would be phased out; snowmobiles would not be permitted except where needed for park management, and in Clyde and Bruton townships.

In late autumn 1974, the Algonquin Park Master Plan was released (covering the management period to 1994). Its aims were to maintain the economic base for local communities while continuing to provide Ontario residents with a diversity of recreational opportunities. It established zones like those suggested in the Provisional Plan: Natural Zones, representative of significant habitats; Historic Zones; Recreation Zones, adjacent to Highway 60 and in two locations on the eastern side of the park; a large Primitive Zone, free of logging; and Recreation / Utilization zones in which both recreation and logging could take place.

Interest groups once again expressed concern that their legitimate requests had not been met. Patrick Hardy, of the Algonquin Wildlands League, wrote in comment on the Master Plan, "This was a bitter disappointment to all the citizens' groups. There was no mention of phasing out the logging." Nevertheless, Algonquin had a long-term plan, one that provided for regular reviews every five years, to meet prevailing conditions. In 1978, a reservation system, quota system, and a can and bottle ban were introduced. According to a 1979 report, "56 percent of the plan's directives have been carried out, 15 percent have been initiated, 25 percent have not been implemented, and two percent have been rejected as not being feasible."

A discussion booklet was published, and public hearings were held in spring and summer 1979 to review the plan.

The Provincial Parks Council made 102 recommendations on thirty-five issues, and the Report of the Minister, completed in late 1979, addressed, among other issues, acid rain (only recently recognized as a threat), management of historical resources, motorboats, fish and wildlife management, and logging. A second review — with eight public meetings — was held in 1989. The minister's response to the recommendations was released in June 1991, with a promise of a complete revision of the Master Plan by spring 1992. The goal for the park was "to provide protection of natural and cultural features, continuing opportunities for a diversity of low intensity, recreational, wilderness and natural environmental experiences; and within this provision continue and enhance the park's contribution to the economic, social and cultural life of the region." Additional issues examined included retention of Clyde and Bruton townships and plans to phase out all hunting (which had been permitted in Clyde and Bruton townships since 1961, when they were annexed to the park) by 2010; phasing out motorboats and water-skiing; maintenance of historical resources including archives; addition of trails; a review of the canoe quota system; issues related to the continued logging in the park and more.

Additional reviews on specific topics have taken place by the Provincial Parks Council, between the formal reviews. One such review related to leases in the park. Leasing had been encouraged by the government for almost fifty years, but gradually phased out after 1954. In 1986, following public meetings, and recommendation of the Parks Council, it was decided to extend all leases to end in 2017.

With the approach of the Algonquin Park centennial, a long-standing question threatened a reassessment of the very nature and management of the park: whose land is it?

. . .frequent rocky ridges and deep glens. . ."sugar-loaf" hills, from whose lofty crests the vast expanse of forest can be overlooked. . .
WALTER SHANLEY, 1856

13

TOWARD A SECOND CENTURY

As cars passed through the East Gate of Algonquin Park in August 1988, their occupants were met by peaceful protesters from the Algonquin Golden Lake First Nation. They claimed that Algonquin Park was native land, an assertion that had profound repercussions as Algonquin Park approached its second century.

The history of the land claim dates back over two hundred years. The position of the Algonquins was outlined in the protest information pamphlet:

> The land you are travelling on belongs to the Algonquin people. We have been its guardians for thousands of years. When Europeans first came here, we welcomed them and became partners with them in trade. We have been the Crown's allies since 1760. We fought in most of Britain's wars, here and abroad. In 1763 the King promised us that our land would never be taken except in a formal treaty, and we relied on that promise. We have never made any treaty with Britain or Canada to sell any of our land. Beginning in the 1800s, lumbermen began to cut the white pine forest; they moved up our valley, clearcutting; and the settlers followed them. Our land was taken and our hunting grounds were destroyed by the loggers and settlers, leaving us poor and scattered. Out of the original 3.4 million hectares (8.5 million acres), we have less than 800 (2,000) left.

As noted in Chapter 2, King George III's Proclamation of 1763 deemed to be native land the territories lying west of the colony of Quebec; such territories included some lands now within Algonquin Park. Although lands were to be purchased from the Crown when the natives agreed to cede them, and the lands were to be reserved for native use alone, the territories of the Ottawa watershed soon rang with the sound of axes and the grating of ploughs through the soil. The Crown purchased the lands of Southern Ontario from the Mississaugas — the predominant native population, and victors over the Iroquois in the 1690s. The Mississauga lands extended to the Ottawa River.

Petitions for the lands along both banks of the Ottawa River and its tributaries were repeatedly made by the Algonquins throughout the 1800s. They first asked that incursions into their hunting grounds by loggers and settlers stop, then that they be compensated for lands already settled. In 1836, they learned that part of the lands they claimed had been ceded by the Mississaugas. They then asked for a portion of the payment. Eventually the Algonquins asked for lands in unsettled townships so they might continue their lives as hunters and trappers.

An 1839 report by Mr. Justice Macauley, on behalf of the government of Upper Canada, concluded that an Algonquin claim to the north side of the Ottawa might be justified; however, "pretensions to the south side are more doubtful." In response to an 1840 petition by the Algonquins, T.W. Murdock, chief secretary to Governor General Lord Sydenham, wrote that His Excellency had informed him the Crown was not obliged to pay for lands the Algonquins claimed. Although a few lower status officials occasionally supported the claim in reports, other governors general, both earlier and later, held that it was not the will of the Crown to grant exclusive use of the hunting grounds to any single group.

In 1923, a joint federal-provincial commission investigated claims by the Chippewa and Mississaugas that they had never given up much of their land in Central Ontario. In the 1923 Williams Treaty, the Mississaugas ceded to the Crown hunting and fishing rights and title in lands that included Algonquin Park.

In 1982, Queen Elizabeth II signed the Constitution Act, which "recognized and affirmed" existing aboriginal rights. The following year, the Algonquins again petitioned the governor general for lands on the south shore of the Ottawa River. These lands extend from the Mattawa River to Hawksbury and include Algonquin Park, Parliament Hill and all unoccupied Crown lands. Chief Greg Sarazin asserted that his people, the Algonquins of Golden Lake, still owned the land under the terms of the Royal

Proclamation of George III, as they had never extinguished their rights by treaty.

In 1988, Sarazin, current negotiator for the Algonquins, proposed a settlement to the Canadian and Ontario governments, in the form of sufficient compensation to provide for a self-sufficient, independent economy for the Algonquins. Foremost among the specific proposals was that the Algonquins gradually be given control, administration and operation of Algonquin Park.

In January 1991, the Ontario government dropped charges of trespass and moose hunting in Algonquin Park against Chief Clifford Meness of the Algonquins of Golden Lake. The Honourable C.J. Wildman, minister of Natural Resources and of Native Affairs, said the 1990 Sparrow decision of the Supreme Court of Canada on aboriginal rights "forced" the government to permit native hunting and fishing within Algonquin Park. From then on, natives would be charged only if their hunting and fishing in the park endangered public safety or conservation programs. Mr. Wildman said the Algonquin claim was strong and indicated the government preferred a negotiated settlement. He warned that a court might award the Algonquins full control of the park.

William Calvert, chairman of the Friends of Algonquin Park, said the government position was "probably the most serious setback to conservation in the past 150 years." A native spokesperson countered that animals would be killed only for food and ceremonial uses, and no hunting would take place during the tourist season so as not to have a negative impact on the local economy.

Tourist operators in the Huntsville area joined together with local chambers of commerce, and the Friends of Algonquin Park, forming the Ad Hoc Committee to Save Algonquin Park to protest government action. At a public meeting in May 1991, concern was raised regarding the future of tourism, the validity of the land claim, and the appropriateness of Mr. Wildman holding both Natural Resources and Native Affairs portfolios. However, the committee emphasized that their concerns were not anti-native but pro–Algonquin Park. The government indicated it would begin formal discussions with the natives on June 15 and interim hunting and fishing agreements were being pursued.

A few days after negotiations began, the Ad Hoc Committee spokesperson, Peter Ward, presented a report that disputed the Algonquin claim of occupation since "time immemorial." The Algonquins, the report said, had been forced to leave their lands by the Iroquois in 1649. They had not returned to their former hunting grounds in the upper Ottawa Valley, then in the hands of the Mississaugas, until the late 1700s or early 1800s. The report also challenged the Algonquins' claim to all of Algonquin Park, especially those parts outside the Ottawa Valley. The report outlined additional flaws in the land claim and asked the government to conduct further historical research, to exclude Algonquin Park from any settlement and to suspend negotiations on interim fishing and hunting agreements.

The Golden Lake Algonquins replied that they made no claim to lands outside the Ottawa River watershed and that they had documentation of historical traditional use of the land. Natural Resources Minister Wildman said the government was interested in doing additional research but interim agreements were appropriate. In October 1991, a one-year hunting agreement was negotiated, but no agreement on fishing could be reached.

During the next year, the Ad Hoc Committee issued four reports on aspects of Algonquin Park: the fragile fishery, finances, new historical research and an analysis of the Supreme Court decision in the Sparrow case.

The financial report revealed that the park operates at a multi-million-dollar annual deficit. In order for Algonquin Park to provide an independent self-supporting economy for the Algonquins of Golden Lake, either the government would have to absorb the deficit for them or the Algonquins would be "obliged to bring in radically new revenue-generating activities such as massive new real estate development that, in substance, would destroy Algonquin as a park." A June 1992 fact sheet from the Golden Lake Algonquins stated, however, that:

> The basis of our claim is our inherent right to the land, the harvest of food and resources and the right to govern ourselves. . . . Continued shared access to Algonquin Park, by all, is a fundamental principle that we endorse. . . . It is a natural recreation area and a place of enduring beauty which we would want to share with all of our neighbours. . . . [We] will not allow commercial exploitation of the Park through such activities as strip mining, commercial hunting and fishing or real estate development. Information to the contrary is simply untrue.

The Ad Hoc Committee's historical research held that the lands the Algonquins asserted to be theirs in 1763 were simultaneously claimed by the Iroquois and the Mississaugas, in each case by right of conquest. Previous rejection of the claim by the Crown and other natives and the campaigns of the Mississaugas in the 1690s were reviewed. The committee recommended that "the Golden Lake people be assisted with a meaningful economic program and/or cash and/or some of the . . . Crown Land outside Algonquin Park."

In the report on the Sparrow decision, Peter Ward examined the court's three tests in the British Columbia case. Was an existing aboriginal right being exercised at the time of the Constitution Act of 1982? Was there evidence that occupation by the natives had been continuous? Had previous rights been extinguished by the Crown? The answers to all three had been favourable to the defendant in the Sparrow case; however, the Ad Hoc Committee argued that the Golden Lake Algonquins failed in all three tests. The report concluded that "the Ontario Government was in no way forced by the Sparrow decision to grant special hunting and fishing rights to the Golden Lake people."

Such arguments, however, apply only if the accepted authority is Canada's Supreme Court. In November 1992, Greg Sarazin declared that "Algonquin nation law as it pertains to conservation and our hunting activities has displaced Ontario jurisdiction in that particular area, at least in the interim. . . . When the Europeans first came in contact with the Algonquin People — the French at first — treaties were made, agreements were made and alliances were made in congress of war. Those agreements were made on a nation-to-nation basis. Later the British displaced the French and those agreements were renewed . . . and those were made on a nation-to-nation basis as well. . . . Somehow between then and today that nation-to-nation relationship has been compromised." When Canada comes to the table, negotiations with the Algonquins will be on a nation-to-nation basis, he said.

As 1992 drew to a close, the government of Ontario contracted additional historical research and negotiated a second interim hunting agreement; the federal government upgraded its status from observer to negotiator; and the Algonquins of Golden Lake held that the land claim area comes under Algonquin law.

Other issues also faced Algonquin Park as it approached its centennial. The 1992 master plan revision had not yet been completed. Acid rain, first recognized as a threat in the 1970s, continued to fall on the forests. Tourist mobility brought the gypsy moth to the Algonquin-Muskoka region. The effects of global warming on the plants and animals of the transition zone were as yet unknown.

The old land-use battles continued as well. In 1991, the Algonquin Wildlands League asked that a complete moratorium be placed on logging in Algonquin Park. The Canadian Parks and Wilderness Society asked why Algonquin Park's forestry management plan was approved while revisions to the Park Master Plan were still under review. The Federation of Ontario Naturalists declared the park was being managed by "political expediency."

Throughout its history, Algonquin Provincial Park has faced pressures from outside its boundaries. Governments, park superintendents and individuals have given much thought to the sound management and protection of this park. Today, even more than a century ago, the preservation of the headwaters, forests and wildlife must be a priority. This is not merely a matter of preserving the scenery and the opportunity to experience the park. We are the trustees of these lands for future generations, not only of our own province and country but of the global community to which we belong.

BIBLIOGRAPHY

Note: Some people prefer their history without footnotes or endnotes. Others prefer extensively detailed notes, itemizing every significant point whether quoted directly or not. Publishing requires compromise at times. Consequently, an early manuscript, with endnotes, has been placed in the Algonquin Park Museum Archives.

Abernethy, R. "Do It the Old Way." *The Huntsville Forester*, May 29, 1991.

"An Act to Incorporate the Haliburton, Whitney and Mattawa Railway Company." *Canada Sessional Papers*, 1899.

Adams, J. *Ten Thousand Miles Through Canada*. New York: Frederick Stokes Company, 1912.

Addison, O. *Early Days in Algonquin Park*. Toronto: McGraw-Hill Ryerson Press, 1974.

Addison, O., and E. Harwood. *Tom Thomson — The Algonquin Years*. Toronto: The Ryerson Press, 1969.

"The Algonquin Experience," brochure. Algonquin Park Museum Archives.

"Algonquin Golden Lake First Nation Find Flaws in Ad Hoc Committee's Press Statement." *This Week*, June 25, 1991.

"The Algonquin National Park Act, 1893." *Ontario Sessional Papers*, 1894

Algonquin Park Master Plan. Ontario Ministry of Natural Resources, 1974.

"Algonquin Park Meetings." *North Bay Nugget*, July 26, 1979.

Algonquin Park Will Be a Better Place Because Loggers Have Been There. Canadian Pulp and Paper, September 1969.

Algonquin Provincial Park First Five-Year Review. Ontario Ministry of Natural Resources, 1979.

Algonquin Provincial Park: Interim Guidelines for Planning and Management. Ontario Department of Lands and Forests, 1970.

Algonquin Provincial Park: Master Plan Review 1989–90. Ontario Ministry of Natural Resources, 1991.

Algonquin Provincial Park Provisional Master Plan. Ontario Department of Lands and Forests, 1968.

Algonquin Provincial Park: Public Hearings on the Provisional Master Plan; Summary of Briefs. Department of Lands and Forests, June 1969.

Allen, G. "Halt Urged to Logging in Algonquin." *The Globe and Mail*, March 9, 1991

Anderson, R. Interview by R. Pittaway, February 2, 1977. Algonquin Park Museum Archives.

Baddeley, F.H. "Exploring Report." In F. Murray, *Muskoka and Haliburton 1615–1875*. Toronto: Champlain Society, University of Toronto Press, 1963.

Bain, J.W. "Surveys of a Water Route between Lake Simcoe and the Ottawa River by the Royal Engineers 1819–1827." *Ontario History*, Vol. 50, 1958.

Bartlett, G.W. "Algonquin National Park." Crown Lands Department. *Ontario Sessional Papers*, 1900.

———. "Algonquin Provincial Park," Report of 1915. *Ontario Sessional Papers*, 1916.

———. "Algonquin Provincial Park," Report of 1918. *Ontario Sessional Papers*, 1919.

Baskerville, G. Interview by R. MacKay, January 1976. Algonquin Park Museum Archives.

Bell, A. *The Way to the West*. Barrie, 1991.

Bernard, M. Interview by R. Pittaway, January 27, 1977. Algonquin Park Museum Archives.

Bernier, L. Statement, July 17, 1973.

Bice, R. *Along the Trail with Ralph Bice in Algonquin Park*. Toronto: Consolidated Amethyst Communications Inc., 1980.

———. Interview by R. MacKay, January 18, 1976. Algonquin Park Museum Archives.

Bodsworth, F. "Can They Save Algonquin Park?" *Maclean's*, June 1, 1954.

Borutski, M. Interview by R. MacKay, December 17, 1975. Algonquin Park Museum Archives.

Bouges, C. Interview by R. MacKay, November 23, 1975. Algonquin Park Museum Archives.

Briscoe, H. "Report of a Survey from Lake Simcoe to the Ottawa, 1826." In F. Murray, *Muskoka and Haliburton 1615–1875*. Champlain Society, University of Toronto Press, 1963.

Brunelle, R. *Logging in Algonquin Park*, Statement, April 29, 1969. Master Plan Files, Algonquin Park Museum Archives.

Brunton, D.F. *The Vascular Plant Collections of John Macoun in Algonquin Provincial Park*. Syllogeus No. 21. Ottawa: National Museum of Natural Sciences, 1979.

Burchat, J. Interview by R. MacKay, December 17, 1975. Algonquin Park Museum Archives.

Burke, W.R. "Hints to Surveyors about to Survey a Township for the Ontario Government." *Periodical Proceedings of Association of Ontario Land Surveyors*, No. 7, 1892, Ontario Archives.

Burton, D. Interview by R. Pittaway, January 13, 1977. Algonquin Park Museum Archives.

Byrne, T. Survey of Anglin Township, Report of Commissioner of Crown Lands. *Ontario Sessional Papers*, 1887.

———. Survey of Deacon Township, Report of Commissioner of Crown Lands. *Ontario Sessional Papers*, 1886.

———. Survey of Freswick Township, Report of Commissioner of Crown Lands. *Ontario Sessional Papers*, 1885.

Cain, W.C. *Notice to Timber Licences in Algonquin Provincial Park*, memorandum, February 20, 1939. Algonquin Park Museum Archives.

Callighen, H.A. *Chief Ranger Reports*. H.A. Callighen Papers, Ontario Archives.

Camp Ahmek brochure. Algonquin Park Museum Archives.

Camp Pathfinder brochure. Algonquin Park Museum Archives.

Camp Waubuno brochure. Algonquin Park Museum Archives.

Campbell, G. *The Airplane in Algonquin Park*. Algonquin Park Museum Archives, no date.

"Canadian Pacific Railway: Georgian Bay Branch." *Renfrew Mercury*, December 25, 1874.

Cartright, J. Letter to A. Saunders, April 15, 1946. A.S. Miller files, Algonquin Park Museum Archives.

Case, F. *History of Northway Camp*, 1942. Algonquin Park Museum Archives.

Catty, J.P. "Survey of a Route between Lake Simcoe and the Ottawa, 1819." In E.C. Guillet, *The Valley of the Trent*. Toronto: Champlain Society, University of Toronto Press, 1957.

Chartrand, E. Interview by R. MacKay, March 25, 1976. Algonquin Park Museum Archives.

Clarke, C.H.D. Interview by R. MacKay, December 2, 1975. Algonquin Park Museum Archives.

_____. *The Rosebary Lake Site–Algonquin Park*, typewritten manuscript, 1964. Algonquin Park Museum Archives.

Clouthier, T. Interview by R. MacKay, February 23, 1976. Algonquin Park Museum Archives.

Conway, A. Statement. *Wildland News*, Vol. 1, September 1968.

"Critics to Advise on Park." *The London Free Press*, September 6, 1969.

Crombie, D. Interview by R. Pittaway, January 14, 1977. Algonquin Park Museum Archives.

Cummings, H.R. *Early Days in Haliburton*. Ontario Department of Lands and Forests, 1962.

Dawson, B. *Superb Algonquin Park Fisheries in Danger*. Information Bulletin No. 2, Ad Hoc Committee to Save Algonquin Park, 1991.

Day, G. and B. Trigger. "Algonquin." In *Handbook of North American Indians*, Vol. 15, Smithsonian Institution, 1978.

Dickson, J. *Camping in the Muskoka Region — A Story about Algonquin Park*. Ontario Department of Lands and Forests, 1963. First Printed 1886.

_____. Survey of Bishop Township, Report of Commissioner of Crown Lands. *Ontario Sessional Papers*, 1884.

_____. Survey of Canisbay Township, Report of Commissioner of Crown Lands. *Ontario Sessional Papers*, 1882.

"Don't Ask Us to Starve for Them." *The Eganville Leader*, December 5, 1968.

Duff, J.A. "The Algonquin National Park of Ontario." *Ontario Sessional Papers*, 1901.

Dunne, Alvin. Interview by R. Pittaway, January 25, 1977. Algonquin Park Museum Archives.

Dunne, Aubrey. Interview by R. MacKay, November 22, 1975. Algonquin Park Museum Archives.

Dymond, J.R. Letter to F.A. MacDougall, November 3, 1937. Dymond Files, Royal Ontario Museum Archives.

Edwards, C.A. *Taylor Statten: A Biography*. Toronto: Ryerson Press, 1960.

Eid, L. "The Ojibwa-Iroquois War: The War the Five-Nations Did Not Win." *Ethnohistory*, Vol. 26, 1979.

"Essence of a Natural Environment Park," editorial. *Huntsville Forester*, March 6, 1991.

Fallis, M. Interview by R. Pittaway, February 1, 1977. Algonquin Park Museum Archives.

Fitzgerald, J.W. Survey of Fitzgerald Township, Report of Commissioner of Crown Lands. *Ontario Sessional Papers*, 1886.

_____. Survey of Master Township, Report of Commissioner of Crown Lands. *Ontario Sessional Papers*, 1892.

_____. Survey of Stratton Township, Report of Commissioner of Crown Lands. *Ontario Sessional Papers*, 1893.

_____. Survey of Township of Niven, Report of Commissioner of Crown Lands. *Ontario Sessional Papers*, 1889.

_____. Survey of White Township, Report of Commissioner of Crown Lands. *Ontario Sessional Papers*, 1887.

_____. Survey of Wilkes Township, Report of Commissioner of Crown Lands. *Ontario Sessional Papers*, 1882.

Fowle, C.D. *The Status of the Elk in Algonquin Park*. Ontario Department of Lands and Forests, Wildlife Report No. 63, 1960.

Fowle, D. Interview by R. Pittaway, January 13, 1977. Algonquin Park Museum Archives.

Furlong, G. Interview by R. MacKay, June 4, 1976. Algonquin Park Museum Archives.

Garland, G. *Glimpses of Algonquin*. Friends of Algonquin Park, 1990.

Garvey, Mary. Interview by R. MacKay, February 24, 1976. Algonquin Park Museum Archives.

Garvey, Mike. Interview by R. MacKay, May 1977. Algonquin Park Museum Archives.

Goldblatt, H. *Negotiation Bulletin: The Algonquins of Golden Lake Negotiations*. May 1992.

Golden Lake Band Aboriginal Title Claim Draft Historical Report. Specific Claims Branch, Indian and Northern Affairs, March 1986.

Gorrie, P. "Hunting the Middle Ground." *The Toronto Star*, March 11, 1991.

Gray, T. "Will 1993 Be a Birthday Party or Goodbye?" *The Huntsville Forester*, May 29, 1991.

Greenfield, D.M. *Diary of a Survey of the Madawaska River, 1847*, Ontario Archives.

Hall, C. "Province Not Natives to Maintain Control of Park Says Minister." *The Citizen*, Ottawa, June 20, 1991.

Hamilton, M.G. *The Call of Algonquin: A Biography of a Summer Camp*. Toronto: Ryerson Press, 1958.

Hanes, H. Interview by R. MacKay, January 16, 1976. Algonquin Park Museum Archives.

Hansen, L.C. *Research Report: The Algonquins of Golden Lake Indian Band Land Claim*. Office of Indian Resource Policy, Ministry of Natural Resources, March 4, 1986.

Harding, R. "200 People Come Looking for Algonquin Park Answers." *The Huntsville Herald*, May 29, 1991.

Hardy, P. "The Disgrace of Algonquin Park." *The Living Wilderness*, Vol. 42, December 1978,

Hawkins, W. Map of the Petawawa River, 1837. Ontario Archives.

_____. "Report of the Commissioners on the Survey of the Ottawa River: Report of Mr. Hawkins, Deputy Provincial Surveyor." *Appendix to Journal of the House of Assembly of Upper Canada*, Toronto, 1839.

Hayden, S. *Proposal by Golden Lake Band to Take Over Algonquin Park for their Economic Independence Is Financially Unsound*. Bulletin No. 3, Ad Hoc Committee to Save Algonquin Park, 1992

Helmsley, A. Interview by R. Pittaway, December 21, 1976. Algonquin Park Museum Archives.

Henry, R.C. "Algonquin Park Now a Native Hunting Ground." *Muskoka Advance*, March 3, 1991.

Hessel, P. *The Algonquin Tribe*. Arnprior: Kechesippi Books, 1987.

_____. "The Algonquins of Golden Lake." *The Beaver*, Winter, 1983.

Holmberg, J. Interview by G. Campbell, no date. Algonquin Park Museum Archives.

Howard, R.B. *Report of the Algonquin Park Advisory Committee: September 1969 – July 1973*. July 1973.

Hueston, T.W. Letter to D. Beauprie, March 4, 1971. Master Plan Files, Algonquin Park Museum.

Humber, R. Letter to R. MacKay, 1975.

Hurley, W.M. and I.T. Kenyon. *Algonquin Park Archaeology*. Department of Anthropology, University of Toronto, Research Report No. 3, 1971.

Hyland, H. Interview by R. MacKay, January 23, 1976, and July 7, 1977. Algonquin Park Museum Archives.

Kase, E. Interview by R. MacKay, December, 1975. Algonquin Park Museum Archives.

Keefer, T.C. *The Ottawa*. Montreal, 1854.

_____. "Report of Mr. T.C. Keefer, Upon the Improvements Desirable to Be Made Upon the Works Under His Charge." *Journal of Legislative Assembly Canada*. App. LL, 1847.

Kemsley, R. "Tourism Minister Gets an Earful about Algonquin." *The Huntsville Forester*, April 10, 1991.

_____. "You Made a Mistake 150 Tell Province." *The Huntsville Forester*, May 29, 1991.

Killan, G. *Protected Places: A History of Ontario's Provincial Park System*. Toronto: Dundurn Press, 1993.

Kirkwood, A. *An Act Respecting Algonkin Forest and Park*, manuscript, 1888. Ontario Archives.

_____. *Algonkin Forest and Park: Letter to the Honorable T.B. Pardee M.P.P., Commissioner of Crown Lands*. Toronto: Warwick and Sons, 1886.

_____. *Papers and Reports upon Forestry, Forestry Schools, and Forest Management in Europe, America and the British Possessions, and upon Forests As Public Parks and Sanitary Resorts*, 1892. Ontario Archives.

_____. *Report of the Royal Commission on Forest Reservation and National Park*, 1893. Reprinted Ontario Department of Lands and Forests, 1959.

Kirkwood, A. and J.J. Murphy. *The Undeveloped Lands in Northern and Western Ontario*. Toronto: Hunter Rose and Company, 1878.

Lambert, R.S. and P. Pross, *Renewing Nature's Wealth: A Centennial History*. Ontario Department of Lands and Forests, 1967.

Lavalley, J. Interview by R. Pittaway, December 16, 1976. Algonquin Park Museum Archives.

Leggett, W.C. Interview by R. Pittaway, 1976. Algonquin Park Museum Archives.

Lisk, B. Interview by R. Pittaway, July 25, 1979. Algonquin Park Museum Archives.

Little, W.T. *The Tom Thomson Mystery*. Toronto: McGraw-Hill Ryerson, 1970.

Long, G. "They Did It the Hard Way." *The Muskoka Sun*, June 1988.

Lower, A.R.M. *Great Britain's Woodyard*. Montreal: McGill-Queen's University Press, 1973.

Macdonell, J.R. *Diary, Survey of Petawawa River*, 1848. Ontario Archives.

MacDougall, F.A. *Algonquin District Report*, 1932. Algonquin Park Museum Archives.

_____. *Algonquin District Annual Report*, 1939. Algonquin Park Museum Archives.

_____. "Algonquin Park." *Forestry Chronicle*, Vol. 12, 1935–6.

_____. *Algonquin Provincial Park Plan*, 1934, Algonquin Park Museum Archives.

_____. "Balance between Logging and Recreation." *Algonquin Park Newsletter*, April 20, 1939.

_____. "Multiple Land Use." *Forestry Chronicle*, Vol. 15, 1939.

MacKay, N.J.M. *Over the Hills to Georgian Bay*. Erin, Ontario: Boston Mills Press, 1981.

MacKay, R. "A Chronology of Algonquin Park." Algonquin Park Technical Bulletin No. 8, Friends of Algonquin Park, 1988.

_____. *More Historic Research Indicates That the Golden Lake Claim to Algonquin Park Is Invalid*. Information Bulletin 4, Ad Hoc Committee to Save Algonquin Park, 1992.

MacKey, W. Letter to A.S. Hardy, transcript. In A. [Saunders] Miller Notes, Algonquin Park Museum Archives.

MacLulich, D. Interview by R. Pittaway, November 23, 1976. Algonquin Park Museum Archives.

Macoun, J. Annual Report Geological Survey of Canada. *Canada Sessional Papers*, 1903.

Mac Taggert, K. Article in *The Globe*, November 17, 1937. Transcript in D. Wyatt Notes, Algonquin Park Museum Archives.

"The Man in Our Life." *ASKI*, Ontario Ministry of Natural Resources, 1975.

Map Illustrative of Georgian Bay Branch and Connections, Canadian Pacific Railway, 1875. Ontario Archives.

Martin, N. "The Harkness Laboratory of Fisheries Research." Ontario Department of Lands and Forests, pamphlet 276, 1968

Martin, N. Interview by R. Pittaway, October 29, 1976. Algonquin Park Museum Archives.

McDonald, J.H. *Algonquin Forest District Report*, 1930, Algonquin Park Museum Archives.

McGuey, H. Interview by R. MacKay, February 6, 1976. Algonquin Park Museum Archives.

McGuey, P. Interview by R. MacKay, February 6, 1976. Algonquin Park Museum Archives.

McIntyre, J. Interview by D. Wyatt, March 1, 1971. Algonquin Park Museum Archives.

McNaughton, J. *Diary Relative to the Survey of the Bonnechere River*, 1848. Ontario Archives.

_____. *Field Notes, Survey of Bonnechere River*, 1948. Ontario Archives.

Meeting to Discuss Algonquin Provincial Park, October 13, 1964. Master Plan Files, Algonquin Park Museum Archives.

Miller, A. Interview by R. Pittaway, November 28, 1979. Algonquin Park Museum Archives.

Minnesing brochure. Algonquin Park Museum Archives.

Montgomery, E. Interview by R. MacKay, December 18, 1975. Algonquin Park Museum Archives.

Murray, A. Geological Survey of Canada Report for Year 1853. *Canada Sessional Papers*, No. 52, Ottawa, 1853.

Noble, W.C. "Vision Pits, Cairns and Petroglyphs at Rock Lake, Algonquin Provincial Park." *Ontario Archaeology*, Vol. 11, 1968.

Northway, M. Interview by R. MacKay, November 21, 1975. Algonquin Park Museum Archives.

_____. *Nominigan: The Early Years*. Private printing, 1970.

A Park for People. Algonquin Park Leaseholders Association, 1969.

Perry, R. "Ghost Camp of Opeongo." In *Blue Lake and Rocky Shore: A History of Children's Camping in Ontario*. Toronto: Natural Heritage/Natural History Inc., 1984.

Phipps, R. The Watershed of Eastern Ontario, Forestry Report, 1884. *Ontario Sessional Papers*, No. 4, 1885.

Pimlott, D.H. Interview by R. Pittaway, January 11, 1977. Algonquin Park Museum Archives.

_____. "The Struggle to Save a Park." *Canadian Audubon*, May-June, 1969.

Pimlott, D.H., J.A. Shannon and G.B. Kolenosky. *Ecology of the Timber Wolf*. Ontario Department of Lands And Forests, 1969.

Planning, Development and Management Policy: Algonquin Provincial Park. Master Plan Files, Algonquin Park Museum Archives.

"Provincial Police Arrest 3 More Following Alleged Poaching Fight." *Toronto Star*, November 6, 1936.

Public Meetings Set to Review Leasing of Cottage Lots in Algonquin and Rondeau Provincial Parks, news release. Ministry of Natural Resources, January 13, 1986.

Regehr, T.D. *The Canadian Northern Railway: Pioneer Road of the Northern Prairies 1895-1918*. Toronto: Macmillan of Canada, 1976.

"Return to House of Commons: Georgian Bay Branch." *Canada Sessional Papers*, No. 57, 1877.

Review of Cottage Leasehold Policy: Algonquin and Rondeau Provincial Parks. Provincial Parks Council, 1986.

Robins, J.D. *The Incomplete Anglers*. Toronto: Collins, 1943.

Robinson, M. "Algonquin Provincial Park," (1923). *Ontario Sessional Papers*, 1924.

Roworth, E. "Nice Guys Ruining the Lakes." *The Telegram*, Toronto, August 30, 1969.

Russell, A.J. Accounts of Expenditure on the Ottawa and Opeongo Road for the Year Ending 1856. *Journal Legislative Assembly*, App. 54, 1857.

_____. Return of Expenditures by Private Individuals on Improvements. *Canada Sessional Papers*, App. MMMM, Ottawa, 1853.

Sarazin, Dan. Interview by R. Pittaway, January 26, 1977. Algonquin Park Museum Archives.

Sarazin, G. "Algonquins South of the Ottawa." in B. Richardson, *Drumbeat: Anger and Renewal in Indian Country*. Toronto: Summerhill Press, Assembly of First Nations, 1989.

Saunders, A. *Algonquin Story*. Ontario Department of Lands and Forests, 1946.

Savage, J. *Aquatic Invertebrates: Mortality Due to D.D.T. and Subsequent Re-establishment, Forest Spraying and Some Effects of D.D.T.* Division of Research Biological Bulletin No. 2, Ontario Department of Lands and Forests, 1949.

Sequence of Events — Algonquin Park Master Plan. Master Plan Files, Algonquin Park Museum Archives.

Shanley, W. Survey between Ottawa and Georgian Bay. *Canada Sessional Papers*, App. 5, Ottawa, 1857.

Shirreff, A. "Topographical Notices of the Country Lying between the Mouth of the Rideau and Penetanguishine on Lake Huron." *Literary and Historical Society of Quebec*, Transactions II, Series III, Quebec, 1831.

Shirreff, C. "Observations on the Advantages of a Canal from the Ottawa to Lake Huron with Information Collected Respecting Its Practicability." In F. Murray, *Muskoka and Haliburton 1615–1875*. Toronto: Champlain Society, University of Toronto Press, 1963.

Simpson, J. The Algonquin National Park of Ontario, (1895). *Ontario Sessional Papers*, 1896.

Smith, D.B. "Who Are the Mississauga?" *Ontario History*, Vol. 17, 1975.

Smith, D.G. *Canadian Indians and the Law: Selected Documents 1663-1972*, Carleton Library # 87. Toronto: McClelland and Stewart, 1975.

Some Things You Should Know about the Land Claim of Algonquin Golden Lake First Nation. Algonquin Golden Lake First Nation, 1992.

Speakman, J. Interview by R. MacKay, December 10, 1975. Algonquin Park Museum Archives.

Stewart, A. *Enforcement Direction on Activities of Golden Lake Indians in Algonquin Park*. Memorandum, A. Stewart to R. Christie, Ministry of Natural Resources, January 18, 1991.

Stewart, E. Survey of Edgar Township, Report of Commissioner of Crown Lands. *Ontario Sessional Papers*, 1887.

Strickland, S. *Twenty-Seven Years in Canada West*, 1853. Reprinted M.G. Hurtig Ltd., 1970.

Stringer, D. Interview by R. MacKay, November 25, 1975. Algonquin Park Museum Archives.

Suggestions for Program of Renewable Resources Development. Ontario Department of Lands and Forests, 1954.

Tayler, G.E. "Indians of Algonquin Park — at the Time of Contact — 1600 A.D.," typewritten manuscript, undated. Algonquin Park Museum Archives.

Thompson, D. "Excerpts from David Thompson's Journal of Occurrences from Lake Huron to the Ottawa River." In F. Murray, *Muskoka and Haliburton 1615–1875*. Toronto: Champlain Society, University of Toronto Press, 1963.

_____. "Letter to J.M. Higginson, Provincial Secretary, April 17, 1843." In F. Murray, *Muskoka and Haliburton 1615–1875*. Toronto: Champlain Society, University of Toronto Press, 1963.

Thomson, P. Algonquin National Park, (1894). *Ontario Sessional Papers*, 1895.

_____. Chief Ranger Thomson's Report. *Ontario Sessional Papers*, 1894.

Turner, J.J. Interview by R. MacKay, February, 1976. Algonquin Park Museum Archives.

Valpy, M. "Algonquin Conflict Hard to Resolve." *The Globe and Mail*, April 11, 1991.

Walpole, J. "Report of Survey from Talbot River to the Madawaska, November 1827." In F. Murray, *Muskoka and Haliburton 1615–1875*. Toronto: Champlain Society, University of Toronto Press, 1963.

Ward, E.L. *Algonquin Park Newsletter*, Vol. 10, 1941, Algonquin Park Museum Archives.

Ward, P.N. *Major Flaws in the Golden Lake Land Claim to Algonquin Park*. Information Bulletin No. 1, Ad Hoc Committee to Save Algonquin Park, 1991.

_____. *Ontario Allows Golden Lake Band to Hunt in Algonquin Park in Spite of Supreme Court's Sparrow Decision — Not Because of It*, Information Bulletin No. 5, Ad Hoc Committee to Save Algonquin Park, 1992.

Waters, S. Diary, 1908. Transcript, Algonquin Park Museum Archives.

West, B. *The Firebirds*. Ontario Ministry of Natural Resources, 1974.

White, A. Letter to G.W. Bartlett, July 11, 1914. Transcript in A. [Saunders] Miller Notes, Algonquin Park Museum Archives.

Whitton, C. *A Hundred Years A-fellin'*. Ottawa: Runge Press, 1943.

Wicksteed, B. *Joe Lavally And The Paleface*. Toronto: Collins, 1948.

Wildman, C.J. "Hunting Rights in Algonquin a Unique Issue." *The Toronto Star*, March 9, 1991.

Wilson, J. Mr. James Wilson's Report, *Ontario Sessional Papers*, 1894.

Wright, J.V. *Ontario Prehistory*. Ottawa: National Museums of Canada, 1972.

"The Wrong Recipe for Algonquin Park," editorial. *Muskoka Advance*, March 3, 1991.

Wyatt, D. "A History of the Origins and Development of Algonquin Park." Algonquin Park Task Force, unpublished background paper, 1971.

PHOTOGRAPHIC EQUIPMENT

Canon FIN

20 mm f 2.8

85 mm f 1.8

100 mm f 4 macro

200 mm f 2.8

300 mm f 4

FL bellows

Wista RF 4 × 5 Field Camera
150 mm Nikkor
90 mm f 4.5 Rodenstock
210 mm f 5.6 Rodenstock

FILM

Kodachrome 35 – I.S.O. 25

Kodachrome 120 – I.S.O. 64

Fujichrome 4 × 5 Professional sheet film I.S.O. 50

THE BOSTON MILLS PRESS